FOLK PRAISE

Compiled by
KEVIN MAYHEW

KEVIN MAYHEW
Publishers

ISBN 0 905725 25 5

Compilation © Copyright 1977 by Kevin Mayhew Ltd.

First published in Great Britain in 1977 by
KEVIN MAYHEW LTD
55 Leigh Road
Leigh-on-Sea Essex

Cover design: Paul Chilvers

Music artwork: Eric Welch and Robert Pryor

Printed by E. T. Heron & Co. Ltd., Essex and London

Sing prai- ses to the li- ving God, glo- ry, hal- le- lu - ia.

Come ,a- dore the li- ving God, glo- ry, hal- le - lu - ia. Though

sun and moon may pass a - way his words will e - ver stay. His

pow - er is for - ev - er - more , glo - ry , hal - le - lu - ia .

Chorus

Glo - ry to the Tri - ni - ty . The un - di -

vi - ded U - ni - ty , the Fa - ther , Son and Spi - rit

one , from whom all life and greatness come .

2. And to the living God we sing,
   glory hallelujah.
   Let our love and praises ring,
   glory hallelujah.
   To all his sons he always gives
   his mercy and his love.
   So praise him now for evermore,
   glory hallelujah.

3. And to the God who cannot die,
   glory hallelujah.
   To the living God we cry,
   glory hallelujah.
   He promised to be with us and
   he lives in ev'ry one.
   We love him now for evermore,
   glory hallelujah.

Words and Music: Sebastian Temple

2

Chorus C   F   G

Ring the bells of free - dom, let the cym - bals speak of jus - tice.

C   F   G   C   *fine*

Clap, clap, clap your hands, I'm mov - ing on.

G

Je - sus said:"Now the king - dom's near for the lame can walk and the

C

deaf can hear. The news is good and the mes-sage clear. Won't you

F   G   G7   C   *D.C.*

come with me? I'm mov - ing on."

2. Jesus said: "Won't you follow me,
and I'll open eyes so that you can see
the fruit that hangs on a dying tree.
Won't you come with me? I'm moving on".

3. Jesus said: "I will soon be gone,
but you know I won't be away for long.
When I return I will sing this song.
Won't you come with me? I'm moving on ".

Words: Michael Cockett
Music: Kevin Mayhew

3

Chorus   C   F   C

Rise, and shine, and give God his glo-ry, glo ry. Rise, and shine, and

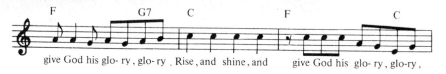

give God his glo-ry, glo-ry. Rise, and shine, and   give God his glo-ry, glo-ry,

chil-dren of   the   Lord. 1. The Lord said to No-ah:"There's gonna be a floody, floody."

Lord said to No-ah:"There's gonna be a floody, floody. Get those child-ren

out of the muddy, muddy,"child-ren of   the   Lord.

2. So Noah, he built him, he built him an arky, arky,
   Noah, he built him, he built him an arky, arky,
   built it out of hickory barky, barky,
   children of the Lord.

3. The animals, they came on, they came on; by twosies, twosies,
   the animals, they came on, they came on, by twosies, twosies,
   elephants and kangaroosies, roosies,
   children of the Lord.

4. It rained and poured for forty daysies, daysies,
   it rained and poured for forty daysies, daysies,
   nearly drove those animals crazyies, crazyies,
   children of the Lord.

5. The sun came out and dried up the landy, landy,
   the sun came out and dried up the landy, landy,
   everything was fine and dandy, dandy,
   children of the Lord.

6. If you get to heaven before I dosies, dosies,
   if you get to heaven before I dosies, dosies,
   tell those angels, I'm comin' toosies, toosies,
   children of the Lord.

Words and Music: Traditional

4

Come, ho - ly Lord, our faith re - new; our lit - tle praise e - nough for you. We ask your mer - cy, Lord, who bear your sa - cred name: your heal- ing touch the glorious bless - ing we can claim.

2. O Jesus come, our hope on earth,
   from heaven you came to share our birth.

3. Come, Spirit blest, our love revive;
   our failing prayer, is made alive.

Words and Music: John Glynn

5

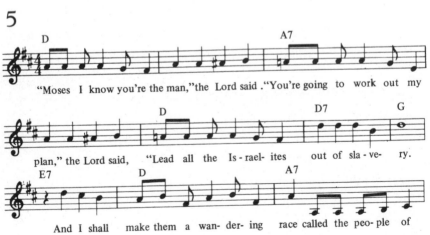

"Moses I know you're the man," the Lord said ."You're going to work out my plan," the Lord said, "Lead all the Is - rael- ites out of sla - ve - ry. And I shall make them a wan- der- ing race called the peo- ple of

| D | D7 | *Chorus* | G | | D | B7 |

God." So ev'-ry day we're on our way, for we're a

| E7 | A7 | D |

tra-vel-ling . wan-der-ing race called the peo-ple of God. ———

2. "Don't get too set in your ways,"
the Lord said.
"Each step is only a phase,"
the Lord said.
"I'll go before you and I shall be a sign
to guide my travelling, wandering race.
You're the people of God."

3. "No matter what you may do,"
the Lord said,
"I shall be faithful and true,"
the Lord said.
"My love will strengthen you as you go along,
for you're my travelling, wandering race.
You're the people of God."

Words and Music: Estelle White

4. "Look at the birds in the air,"
the Lord said.
"They fly unhampered by care,"
the Lord said.
"You will move easier if
you're travelling light,
for you're a wandering, vagabond race.
You're the people of God."

5. "Foxes have places to go,"
the Lord said.
"But I've no home here below,"
the Lord said.
"So if you want to be with me
all your days,
keep up the moving and travelling on.
You're the people of God."

This song may be sung as a round

6

G

Now Je - sus said:"You must love one a- no- ther , pass it

on, pass it on, "And Je- sus said :"Call all men your bro - ther ,come to

me , learn to love , pass it on, pass it on ".

2. So Peter said:
"You must love one another. . .

3. The people said. . .

4. My Father said . . .

5. Now I can say. . .

Words: Michael Cockett
Music: Kevin Mayhew

Oh, Lord my God, how great you are, and yet you care for me. Christ came while I was deep in sin; he came to set me free. You did not send him here to us to fill us all with shame, but that we all might live for ev - er; this is why he came.

2. He came for sinners, not for saints, for they could not believe,
   that he was God and he could give and that they must receive
   forgiveness, life and peace from him who held love in his hands,
   and nailed that love upon a cross for peoples of all lands.

3. And love is still upon that cross wherever there is pain.
   Where hatred rules in cruelty he's crucified again.
   Up Calv'rys made of mounds of food whilst others starve to death
   he drags the cross of selfishness and suffers with each breath.

4. He needs our hands to do his work, he needs our voice to share
   in all the joy his good news brings; he needs our love to care.
   We need his truth deep in our heart, we need his power too.
   We need you, Jesus, Lord of life; we'll suffer now with you.

Words and Music: Gillian Simpson

Oh Lord, my God, when I in awesome won-der, con-si-der
all the worlds thy hand has made, I see the stars, I hear the rolling
thun-der, thy pow'r through-out the un-i-verse dis-played.

Chorus

Then sings my soul, my Saviour God to thee: How great thou
art, how great thou art. Then sings my soul, my Sa-viour God, to
thee: How great thou art, how great thou art.

2. And when I think that God, his Son not sparing,
sent him to die, I scarce can take it in
that on the cross, my burden gladly bearing,
he bled and died to take away my sin.

3. When Christ shall come with shout of acclamation
and take me home, what joy shall fill my heart;
when I shall bow in humble adoration,
and there proclaim; my God, how great thou art.

Words Unknown   Music: Russian Folk Melody

9

Col- ours of day dawn in- to the mind, the sun has come

up, the night is be- hind. Go down in the ci- ty,

in - to the street, and let's give the mes- sage to the peo- ple we

Chorus

meet. So light up the fire and let the flame

burn, o- pen the door, let Je- sus re- turn. Take

seeds of his Spi- rit, let the fruit grow, tell the

peo- ple of Je- sus, let his love show.

2. Go through the park, on into the town;
the sun still shines on, it never goes down.
The light of the world is risen again;
the people of darkness are needing our friend.

3. Open your eyes, look into the sky,
the darkness has come, the sun came to die.
The evening draws on, the sun disappears,
but Jesus is living, and his Spirit is near.

Words and Music: Sue McClellan, John Pac and Keith Ryecroft

The Lord is my true Shep-herd, I have ev'-ry-thing I need, ev'-ry-thing I need he gives to me. He lets me rest in meadow grass and leads me to calm streams, he helps me do what honours him the most.

Chorus

Ev-en when I walk in-to the val-ley dark and cold nev-er will I fear, for you are near. With your hand in mine to guard me, guid-ing all the way. Lord you are my rock, my strength, my life.

2. His arms are open to me, I am welcomed as his guest,
   blessings flow abundant on my head.
   Unfailing kindness in his gift to me through all my life;
   I hope to live with him for evermore.

Words and Music: Peter Madden

In bread we bring you, Lord, our bo-dies' la-bour.
In wine we of-fer you our spi-rits' grief. We do not
ask you, Lord, who is my neigh-bour? But stand u-
ni-ted now, one in be-lief. Oh we have glad-ly heard
your Word, your ho-ly Word, and now in ans-wer, Lord,
our gifts we bring. Our sel-fish hearts make true, our fail-ing
faith re-new, our lives be-long to you, our Lord and King.

2. The bread we offer you is blessed and broken,
   and it becomes for us our spirits' food.
   Over the cup we bring your Word is spoken;
   make it your gift to us, your healing blood.
   Take all that daily toil plants in our heart's poor soil
   take all we start and spoil, each hopeful dream,
   the chances we have missed, the graces we resist,
   Lord, in thy Eucharist, take and redeem.

Words and Music: Kevin Nichols

Chorus

Sing to the Lord for he has triumphed glo-rious-ly.
Horse and the ri-der he has thrown in-to the sea.
1. Sing to the God of glo-ry, sing to the God of ar-mies,
sing to the God who tri-umphs ov-er all our foes.

2. Sing to the Son of Heaven,
sing to the Son in glory,
sing to the Son of Man
who conquers all our foes.

3. Sing to the Holy Spirit,
sing to the Cloud of Glory,
sing to the Advocate
who silences our foes.

Words and Music: Gerald O'Mahony

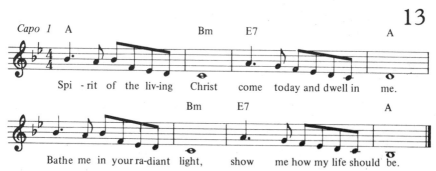

Capo 1

Spi-rit of the liv-ing Christ come today and dwell in me.
Bathe me in your ra-diant light, show me how my life should be.

2. Give me courage from above,
give me hands outstretched to help.
May your searing flame of love,
burn from me the thought of self.

3. Holy Spirit make me hear,
help me listen to your Word.
Make me truthful, free from fear,
graciously to serve the Lord.

Words and Music: Estelle White

Ev'ry lit-tle bird that flies, ev'ry bee in hon-eyed hive, ev'-ry fruit-ful bough a-gainst the au-tumn sky are me-lo-dies born in the breath-tak-ing song of your love, and now I'll sing you the me-lo-dies you taught me, your love-song, the day long with you, the old songs of love that you al-ways re-new.

2. Ev'ry frosty winter dawn,
   ev'ry snowflake floating down,
   ev'ry waiting flower
   within the hardened ground . . .

3. Birds upon returning wing,
   shoots that herald waiting Spring,
   ev'ry blade of grass
   that rustles in the wind . . .

Words: Michael Cockett
Music: Kevin Mayhew

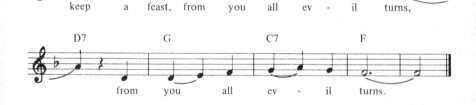

Hail Ma - ry, mo - ther of our God, a lamp that
al - ways burns; for you the an - gels
keep a feast, from you all ev - il turns,
from you all ev - il turns.

2. It's thanks to you God's only Son
   in darkness shed his light;
   it's thanks to you that sinful man
   rejoiced to know what's right,
   rejoiced to know what's right.

3. You gave a place within your womb
   to him who knows no bound;
   a virgin yet a mother too,
   in you his home he found,
   in you his home he found.

4. It's thanks to you creation came
   to know what's good and true;
   God calls his servant 'mother' now—
   no other maid but you,
   no other maid but you!

Words: Willard F. Jabusch
Music: Austrian melody (1649)

16

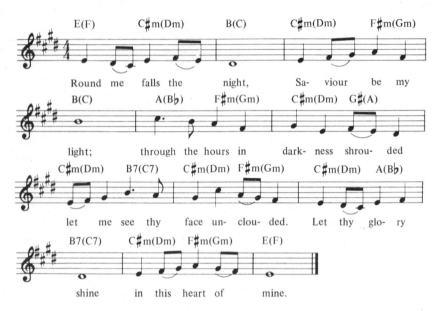

E(F)   C♯m(Dm)   B(C)   C♯m(Dm)   F♯m(Gm)

Round me falls the night, Sa- viour be my

B(C)   A(B♭)   F♯m(Gm)   C♯m(Dm)   G♯(A)

light; through the hours in dark- ness shrou- ded

C♯m(Dm) B7(C7) C♯m(Dm) F♯m(Gm)   C♯m(Dm) A(B♭)

let me see thy face un- clou- ded. Let thy glo- ry

B7(C7) C♯m(Dm) F♯m(Gm)   E(F)

shine in this heart of mine.

2. Earthly work is done,
   earthly sounds are none;
   rest in sleep and silence seeking,
   let me hear thee softly speaking;
   in my spirit's ear
   whisper: "I am near".

3. Blessed heav'nly light
   shining through earth's night;
   voice that oft' of love has told me,
   arms, so strong, to clasp and hold me;
   thou thy watch will keep,
   Saviour o'er my sleep.

Words: W. Romanis   Music: Mary Kennedy

17

E   A   E   B7   E   E7

Search me, oh God, and know my heart to-day.

A   E C♯m F♯7   B   B7

Try me, oh Sa - viour, know my thoughts I pray.

See if there be some sin-ful way in me.
Cleanse me from ev'-ry fault and set me free.

Words: J. Edwin Orr   Music: Maori melody

18

Sea - sons come, sea - sons go, moon - struck
tides will ebb and flow; when I for - get my
con - stant one he draws me back, he brings me home.
Oh love, my love, I hear you far a - way,
a dis - tant storm that will re - fresh the day.

2. Seasons come, seasons go,
   petals fall though flowers grow;
   and when I doubt love lifts a hand
   and scatters stars like grains of sand.
   Oh love, my love, I see you passing by
   like birds that fearlessly possess the sky.

3. Seasons come, seasons go,
   times to reap and times to sow;
   but you are love, a fruitful vine,
   in ev'ry season yielding wine.
   I hear my love in laughter and in song,
   no day too short, no winter night too long.

Words: Michael Cockett
Music: Kevin Mayhew

19

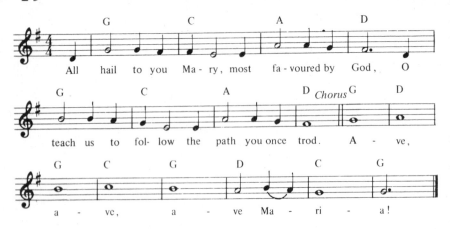

All hail to you Ma - ry, most fa - voured by God, O teach us to fol- low the path you once trod. A - ve, a - ve, a - ve Ma - ri - a!

2. When Gabriel had spoken
you humbly said "Yes".
May we have the courage
God's word to confess.

3. To those for whom sickness
and sadness are near,
show Jesus your first-born,
our Saviour from fear.

4. With Joseph your husband
you cared for our Lord,
guide parents and children
to life's one reward.

5. You treasured, dear mother,
the truth God revealed.
By seeking true wisdom
our faith will be sealed.

6. You spoke at the wedding
and Christ gave them wine.
He now gives his people
the true bread divine.

7. We trustfully echo
the prayer of your Son
that all of God's children
may love and be one.

8. In anguish enfolded
are mother and Son.
By sharing their passion
our victory is won.

9. When Christ died he gave you
as mankind's new Eve.
Inspire all your children
to love, hope, believe.

10. God's life was your living
with him you found peace.
May his loving presence
in us find increase.

Words: David Konstant   Music: Malcolm Campbell-Carr

20

All is qui - et, all is som - bre, from the depths a cry of won - der: Christ is ri - sen! Christ is ri - sen!

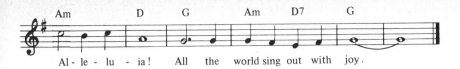

Al - le - lu - ia! All the world sing out with joy.

2. Men upon the road, now mournful,
recognise him in bread broken.

3. Tell the world the good news story,
spread the word of God's great glory.

Words and Music: Peter Madden

21

Come, Christ - ian peo- ple, take heed what I say:

Here, in this sta- ble, your King was born to- day.

Chorus

Star of wis- dom, Child of glad- ness, tell him all your trou -bles.

Ma- ry's boy has banished sadness, why be sorrowful now?

2. Not much to look at
— simply straw and hay —
yet on that carpet
your King was laid today.

3. Man, are you listening?
Take heed what I say:
Here on this planet
your King still lives today.

Words and Music: John Glynn

22

Oh Ma-ry, gen-tle one, teach us to love your Son.

Oh Ma-ry, hum-ble one, help us to serve him.

Chorus

Teach us to ans-wer him, as once you an-swered him:

"Let it be done to me ac-cor-ding to your Word".

2. Oh Mary, peaceful one,
   help us to know your Son.
   Oh Mary, hopeful one,
   teach us to trust him.

3. Oh Mary, grateful one,
   teach us to thank your Son.
   Oh Mary, joyful one,
   help us to praise him.

Words and Music: Francesca Leftley

23

Oh my Lord, you look at me and know me ev'-ry moment of each day. Whe-ther I walk or stand or lie you read my sec-ret thoughts from far a-way.

2. Where could I go to escape your spirit?
   Where could I evade your eyes?
   If I should climb the heights of heaven
   or lie beneath the earth you're by my side.
3. If I flew to where the sun was rising,
   crossed the sea out to the west,
   your hand would still be guiding me,
   your right arm holding me against your breast.
4. If I asked the darkness to surround me,
   and the clouds to be a veil,
   your love would pierce the blackest night,
   your radiance turning it to brightest day.
5. It was you who moulded me and formed me
   when inside the womb I lay;
   for everything I thank you, Lord,
   and for the wonder of myself give praise.

Words (based on Psalm 139) and Music: Estelle White

24

Oh sin-ner man, where you going to run to? Oh, sin-ner man, where you going to run to? Oh, sin-ner man, where you going to run to? all on that day?

2. Run to the moon, moon won't you hide me?
   Run to the sea, sea won't you hide me?
   Run to the sun, sun won't you hide me?
   all on that day.

3. Lord said: "Sinner Man, the moon'll be a-bleeding."
   Lord said: "Sinner Man, the sea'll be a-sinking."
   Lord said: "Sinner Man, the sun'll be a-freezing."
   all on that day.

4. Run to the Lord: "Lord, won't you hide me?". . .

5. Lord said: "Sinner Man, you should have been a-praying!". . .

Words and Music: Traditional

God de- lights in his chil- dren,
clap your hands, O chil- dren of the Lord. God de-
lights in his chil — dren , clap your hands, O chil-dren of the Lord.
(clap) (stamp)
Clap your hands, stamp your feet, raise your voic- es for
life is sweet! God de- lights in his chil- dren,
we're the chil-dren of the Lord.

2. God's in love with his children. . . 5. God gives life to his children. . .

3. God forgives all his children. . .

4. God gives hope to his children. . .   *Words and Music: Estelle White*

This song is very effective if verse 1 is played in F, verse 2 in G, modulating by one bar of D7, verse 3 in A, modulating by one bar of E7, verse 4 in B, modulating by one bar of — F♯7, and verse 5 in C, modulating by one bar of G7.

He is ri - sen, tell the sto - ry to the na - tions of the

night; from their sin and from their blindness, let them walk in Eas - ter

light. Now be - gins a new cre - a - tion, now has come our true sal -

va - tion, Je - sus Christ, the Son of God!

2. Mary goes to tell the others of the wonders she has seen;
   John and Peter come a'running - what can all this truly mean?
   O Rabboni, Master holy, to appear to one so lowly!
   Jesus Christ, the Son of God!

3. He has cut down death and evil, he has conquered all despair;
   he has lifted from our shoulders all the weight of anxious care.
   Risen Brother, now before you, we will worship and adore you,
   Jesus Christ, the Son of God!

4. Now get busy, bring the message, so that all may come to know
   there is hope for saint and sinner, for our God has loved us so.
   Ev'ry church bell is a'ringing, ev'ry Christian now is singing,
   Jesus Christ, the Son of God!

Words: Willard F. Jabusch
Music: Polish melody

Chorus

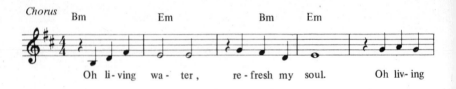

Oh li-ving wa-ter, re-fresh my soul. Oh liv-ing

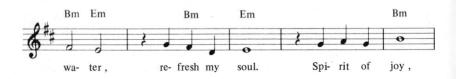

wa-ter, re-fresh my soul. Spi-rit of joy,

Lord of cre-a-tion. Spi-rit of hope. Spi-rit of

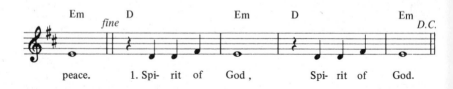

peace. 1. Spi-rit of God, Spi-rit of God.

2. Oh set us free,
   oh set us free.

3. Come, pray in us,
   come, pray in us.

Words and Music: Rosalie Vissing

God gave his Son for sin - ful men, God came and

walked the earth. God went to death on

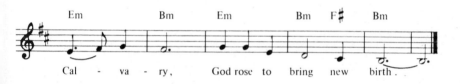

Cal - va - ry, God rose to bring new birth.

2. I know Christ died that all might live,
that all men might be free.
But do I think to tell myself
that Jesus died for me?

3. "Hosanna to the Lord of Hosts",
with all the rest I cried.
But I was too the first to say:
"He must be crucified".

4. And from my mouth came spit so vile
that trickled down his brow.
I screamed those angry mocking words.
I taunted with the crowd.

5. Mine was the hand that held the nail
that bit through bone and flesh.
I rammed the cross into the ground.
I gave him up to death.

6. O mine, dear Lord, mine was the guilt,
mine was the load of pain,
you carried right to Calvary,
that I might live again.

7. I see the love-marks on you now,
your hands, your feet, your side.
I know, Lord, 'twas my lack of love
that had you crucified.

8. There's nothing I can do, my Lord,
to pay back what you've done.
But I need your forgiveness, Lord.
Lord, to your feet I come.

9. Lord, I believe you died for me
to save me from my sin.
I'm sorry, Lord for all I've done.
Come, cleanse me now within.

10. I praise you for your gift of grace
that I can never earn.
Lord, I don't want to sin again.
O help me, Lord, to learn.

Words and Music: Gillian Simpson

29

Sha - lom, my friend, sha - lom my friend, sha - lom, sha - lom. The

peace of Christ I give you today. Sha - lom, sha - lom.

Words: Sandra Joan Billington   Music: Israeli Melody

30

Show me thy ways, oh Lord; re - veal thy -

self to me. I've seen the signs and

won - ders, but Lord, I would know thee.

Words and Music: Traditional

31

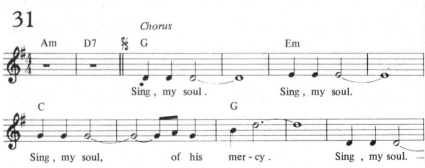

Chorus

Sing, my soul. Sing, my soul.

Sing, my soul, of his mer - cy. Sing, my soul.

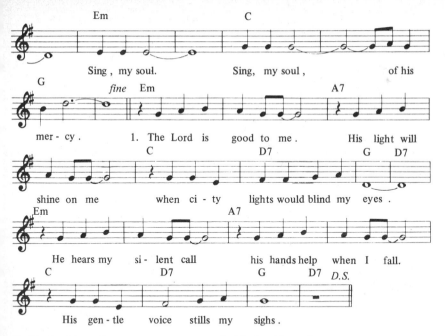

Sing, my soul. Sing, my soul, of his mer-cy.

fine

1. The Lord is good to me. His light will shine on me when ci-ty lights would blind my eyes. He hears my si-lent call his hands help when I fall. His gen-tle voice stills my sighs.

D.S.

2. The Lord is good to me.
His word will set me free
when men would tie me to the ground.
He mocks my foolish ways
with love that never fails.
When I'm most lost then I'm found.

3. The Lord is good to me.
I hear him speak to me.
His voice is in the rain that falls.
He whispers in the air
of his unending care.
If I will hear, then he calls.

Words: Michael Cockett   Music: Estelle White

32

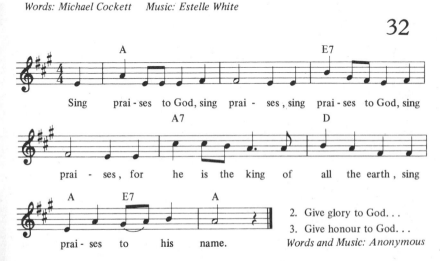

Sing prai-ses to God, sing prai-ses, sing prai-ses to God, sing prai-ses, for he is the king of all the earth, sing prai-ses to his name.

2. Give glory to God...
3. Give honour to God...

Words and Music: Anonymous

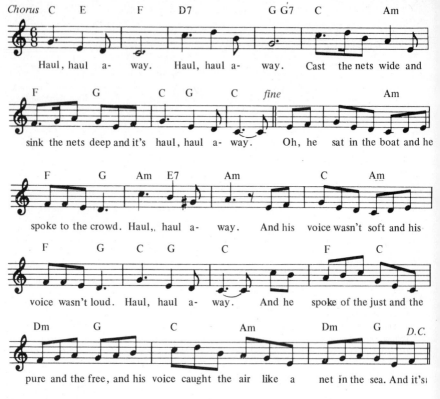

Haul, haul a- way. Haul, haul a- way. Cast the nets wide and sink the nets deep and it's haul, haul a- way. Oh, he sat in the boat and he spoke to the crowd. Haul, haul a- way. And his voice wasn't soft and his voice wasn't loud. Haul, haul a- way. And he spoke of the just and the pure and the free, and his voice caught the air like a net in the sea. And it's...

2. He said: "Cast your nets wide where the water is deep".
   Haul, haul away.
   "Oh, cast the nets wide and sink the nets deep."
   Haul, haul away.
   "Though we've worked through the night and we've nothing to show,
   we will try once again just because you say so."
   And it's...

3. Oh the catch it was huge and the boat it was small.
   Haul, haul away.
   His friends came to help when they heard Peter call.
   Haul, haul away.
   "You must leave us," said Peter, "for we're men of sin."
   But he said: "Come with me and be fishers of men".
   And it's...

Words: Michael Cockett
Music: Kevin Mayhew

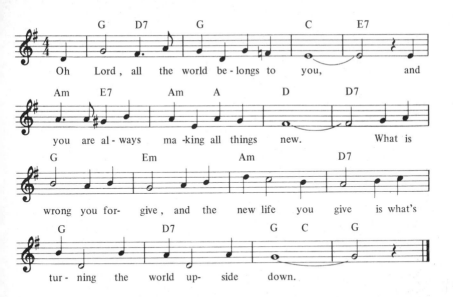

Oh Lord, all the world be-longs to you, and
you are al-ways ma-king all things new. What is
wrong you for- give, and the new life you give is what's
tur-ning the world up- side down.

2. The world's only loving to its friends,
   but you have brought us love that
   never ends;
   loving enemies too,
   and this loving with you
   is what's turning the world upside down.

3. This world lives divided and apart.
   You draw all men together and we start
   in your body to see
   that in fellowship we
   can be turning the world upside down.

4. The world wants the wealth to live in state,
   but you show us a new way to be great;
   like a servant you came,
   and if we do the same,
   we'll be turning the world upside down.

5. Oh Lord, all the world belongs to you,
   and you are always making all things new.
   Send your Spirit on all
   in your Church whom you call
   to be turning the world upside down.

Words and Music: Patrick Appleford

God's spi-rit is in my heart. He has called me and
set me a - part. This is what I have to do,
what I have to do. He sent me to
give the Good News to the poor, tell prisoners that they are
prisoners no more, tell blind peo-ple that they can see,
and set the down trod-den free, and go
tell ev'-ry one the news that the King-dom of
God has come, and go tell ev'-ry-one the
news that God's king-dom has come.

2. Just as the Father sent me,
   so I'm sending you out to be
   my witnesses throughout the world,
   the whole of the world.

3. Don't carry a load in your pack,
   you don't need two shirts on your back.
   A workman can earn his own keep,
   can earn his own keep.

4. Don't worry what you have to say,
   don't worry because on that day
   God's spirit will speak in your heart,
   will speak in your heart.

Words: Alan Dale
Music: Hubert Richards

36

Gon-na lay down my sword and shield down by the riv-er side, down by the riv-er-side, down by the riv-er-side. Gonna lay down my sword and shield down by the riv-er-side. I ain't gon-na stu-dy war no more. I ain't gon-na stu-dy war no more, I ain't gonna stu-dy war no more, I ain't gon-na stu-dy war no more. I ain't gon-na stu-dy war no more, I ain't gonna stu-dy war no more, I ain't gon-na stu-dy war no more.

2. Gonna walk with the Prince of Peace...

3. Gonna shake hands around the world...

Words and Music: Traditional Spiritual

O my Lord, with- in my heart pride will have no
home, eve-ry tal- ent that I have comes from you a-
lone. And like a child at rest close to it's
mo-ther's breast, safe in your arms my soul is calmed.

2. Lord, my eyes do not look high
   nor my thoughts take wings,
   for I can find treasures in
   ordinary things.

3. Great affairs are not for me,
   deeds beyond my scope,
   in the simple things I do
   I find joy and hope.

Words and Music: Estelle White

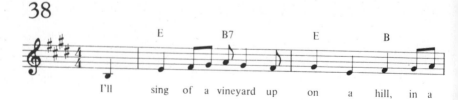

I'll sing of a vineyard up on a hill, in a

fruit-ful land; my be - lov- ed's it was to tend and to till with his

own sweet hand, with his own sweet hand.

2.
A fence he put round it, and in rich soil
planted vines so choice;
the ground would resound with his patient toil
and his mirthful voice,
and his mirthful voice.

3.
A winepress and tower he built with care
while his song was sung,
but when harvest came on the branches there,
only wild grapes hung,
only wild grapes hung.

4.
The world was in darkness and black the sun
as he asked of you:
"What more for my vineyard could I have done
that I did not do,
that I did not do?"

5.
"I'll tear down my vineyard," he cried in pain,
"the new hedge I'll burn;
"where grapes will not grow, there'll be thorns again,
and no rain return,
and no rain return."

6.
"O Israel, my darling," the owner said,
"you have pierced me through,
for I am the Lord you promised to wed,
and that vine is you,
and that vine is you."

Words and Music: Peter de Rosa

39

In his days jus - tice shall flour - ish and peace,

'till the moon shall fail. In his days, sor - row will

van - ish and tears will be wiped a - way.

2. When he comes, caring will conquer
with joy like the rising sun.
When he comes, those who are serving
will rest, as the day is done.

3. And with awe all things will praise him
and sing with the stars above.
Then at last mankind will welcome
and share in his great gift of love.

Words and Music: Francesca Leftley

40

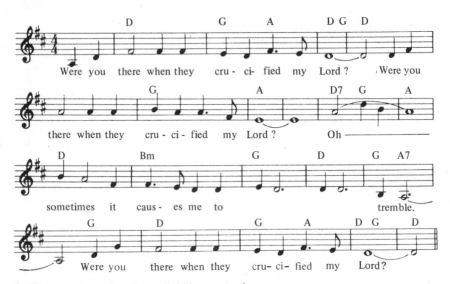

Were you there when they cru-ci-fied my Lord? Were you
there when they cru-ci-fied my Lord? Oh —
sometimes it caus-es me to tremble.
Were you there when they cru-ci-fied my Lord?

2. Were you there when they nailed him to a tree?
   Were you there when they nailed him to a tree?
   Oh, sometimes it causes me to tremble, tremble, tremble.
   Were you there when they nailed him to a tree?
3. Were you there when they pierced him in the side?
4. Were you there when the sun refused to shine?
5. Were you there when they laid him in the tomb?
6. Were you there when he rose from out the tomb?   *Words and Music: Negro Spiritual*

41

What a joy, what a joy for us to say:"We're on our way to the house of the
Lord!" What a joy, what a joy for us to say:"We're on our way to the house of the
Lord!"   1. Com-ing to Je-ru-sa-lem, on this ho-ly ground,

ci - ty mounted on a hill, its hous-es all a - round.

2. All the tribes of Israel,
   countless caravans,
   everyone is going there
   to where the temple stands.

4. Here within your walls a man
   may be safe at last.
   City of my happy heart,
   a fortress holding fast.

3. Through your gates we'll enter in
   open wide the door.
   Here we'll find a welcome place
   and peace for evermore.

5. Dearest name of all my friends,
   may you prosper still.
   Standing like a sentinel
   on Zion's royal hill.

Words (based on Psalm 122) and Music: Willard F. Jabusch

42

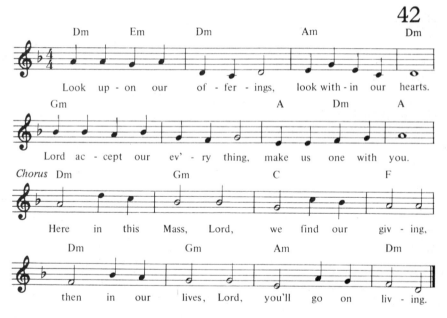

Look up-on our of - fer - ings, look with-in our hearts.

Lord ac - cept our ev' - ry thing, make us one with you.

Chorus

Here in this Mass, Lord, we find our giv - ing,

then in our lives, Lord, you'll go on liv - ing.

2. What have we to offer you, Lord of heaven and earth?
   Lord, accept our nothingness, make us one with you.

*Adapted from a Mariapolis
version of the Focolari*

43

God   is   love   and the   one who lives in love lives in

God, and God   lives in   him.   God   is love and the

one who lives in love lives in   God, and God lives in   him.   And

we have come to know and have be-   lieved   the

love which God has for   us.   God is love and the

one who lives in love lives in   God, and God lives in   him.

2. God is hope. . .

3. God is peace. . .

4. God is joy. . .

Words and Music: Anonymous

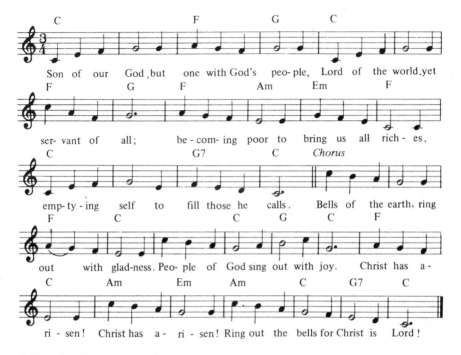

Son of our God, but one with God's peo-ple, Lord of the world, yet
ser-vant of all; be-com-ing poor to bring us all rich-es,
emp-ty-ing self to fill those he calls. Bells of the earth, ring
out with glad-ness. Peo-ple of God sing out with joy. Christ has a-
ri-sen! Christ has a-ri-sen! Ring out the bells for Christ is Lord!

2. Humbling himself to come here among us,
   dying our death to bring us new life,
   shepherd of all yet lamb to the slaughter,
   coming down low to lift us up high.

3. Love sent him down as friend and as brother,
   sharing our life to give us his own,
   sharing our hell to bring us to heaven,
   one with the homeless, leading us home.

4. Bearing our cross to lighten our burden,
   crowned then with thorns to make us all kings,
   stripped and reviled to clothe us in glory,
   crying "I thirst", refreshing all things.

5. Breathing his last to send us his Spirit,
   sealed in a tomb to open man's grave,
   guarded by men to rescue and free us,
   sinking with us, to rise and to save.

6. Light of the world, yet buried in darkness,
   rising again to shine like the sun,
   feeling our coldness to warm and cherish,
   to have and hold us, with him now one.

Words and Music: Michael Evans

45

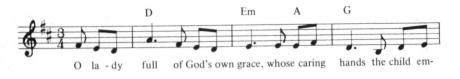

O la-dy full of God's own grace, whose caring hands the child em-

braced, who listened to the Spi-rit's word, be-lieved and trus-ted in the

Chorus

Lord. O vir-gin fair, star of the sea, my dear-est moth-er pray for

me. O vir-gin fair, star of the sea, my dear-est moth-er, pray for me.

2. O lady who felt daily joy
   in caring for the holy boy,
   whose home was plain and shorn of wealth,
   yet was enriched by God's own breath.

3. O lady who bore living's pain
   but still believed that love would reign,
   who on a hill watched Jesus die
   as on the cross they raised him high.

4. O lady who, on Easter day,
   had all your sorrow wiped away
   as God the Father's will was done
   when from death's hold he freed your Son.

Words and Music: Estelle White

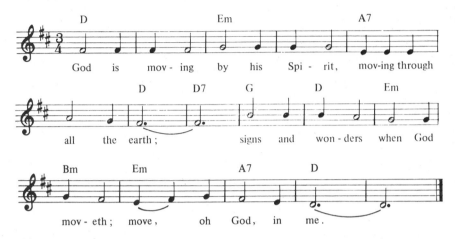

God is mov-ing by his Spi-rit, mov-ing through all the earth; signs and won-ders when God mov-eth; move, oh God, in me.

Words and Music: Anonymous

47

Jan-u-a-ry brings the snow, and the white frost glis-tens; I'm a child full of love, speak, Lord, and I'll lis-ten.

2. March means sun and wind and rain,
   springtime flowers dancing,
   I am young, growing fast,
   wanting all the answers.

3. Maytime blossoms fill the air,
   here's a time for pleasure!
   Keep me safe, O my Lord,
   in my work and leisure.

4. In July the trees are tall,
   butterflies are roving.
   In my prime, may I be
   faithful in my loving.

5. In September's golden fields
   harvesters are reaping,
   and my mind gathers in
   mem'ries worth the keeping.

6. In November there are mists
   jewelling the grasses.
   Now my steps lose their spring;
   how each moment passes!

7. Come December days grow short
   and they say my life's through;
   but, my Lord, it's been good,
   and I want to thank you.

Words and Music: Estelle White

48

The Mass is end-ed, all go in peace.
We must di-min-ish, and Christ in-crease.

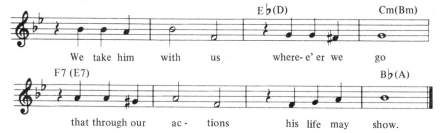

We take him with us where-e'er we go

that through our ac - tions his life may show.

2. We witness his love to ev'ryone
   by our communion with Christ the Son.
   We take the Mass to where men may be,
   so Christ may shine forth for all to see.

3. Thanks to the Father who shows the way.
   His life within us throughout each day.
   Let all our living and loving be
   to praise and honour the Trinity.

4. The Mass is ended, all go in peace.
   We must diminish and Christ increase.
   We take him with us where e'er we go
   that through our actions his life may show.

Words and Music: Sebastian Temple

49

The rain came Knock-ing on the win - dow pane. The

rain came knocking on the win-dow pane. The rain came knocking on the

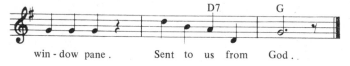

win - dow pane . Sent to us from God . .

2. The stars came twinkling in the darkened sky. (3)
   Sent to us from God.

3. The sun came shining through the open door. . .

4. The flowers came peeping through the green, green grass. . .

5. The lambs came frisking in the open fields. . .

6. The babes came smiling in their mothers' arms. . .

Words and Music: Sister M. Pereira

50

Good La - dy Pov - er - ty, come be my bride;
for - ev - er you and me, walk side by side.
Teach me your wis - dom, lead me your way.
Show me the path you take and walk with Christ each day.

2. Good Lady Poverty, so filled with grace;
   such sweet humility shines from your face.
   You have no pride or vanity.
   Great daughter of the Lord, his love has made you free.

3. Good Lady Poverty, I sing your praise.
   St. Francis, blessed one, has walked your ways.
   He sang your virtues; you were his prize.
   Good Lady Poverty, an angel in disguise.

Words and Music: Sebastian Temple

51

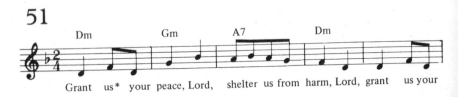

Grant us* your peace, Lord, shelter us from harm, Lord, grant us your

peace, Lord, shield us with your love. Just as a fath - er
cares for his chil – dren grant us your peace, Lord, shield us with your love.

*or them

2. Grant us your strength, Lord,
   shelter us from harm, Lord,
   grant us your strength, Lord,
   shield us with your love.
   From dusk till daybreak, each hour of each day,
   grant us your strength, Lord,
   shield us with your love.

Words: Francesca Leftley
Music: Israeli Folk Song (arr. Francesca Leftley)

52

Hail Ma-ry full of grace, the Lord is with thee,
bless-ed art thou a-mong wo- men and bless - ed is the fruit of thy womb,
Je - sus. Ho - ly Ma - ry, mo-ther of God, pray for us
sin - ners now and at the hour of our death. A - men.

Words: Traditional   Music: Estelle White

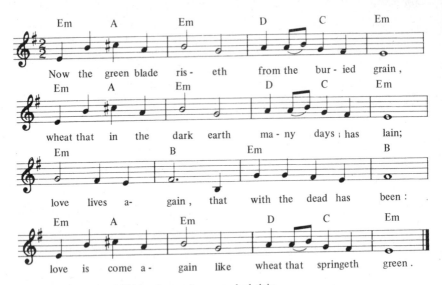

Now the green blade ris - eth from the bur - ied grain,
wheat that in the dark earth ma - ny days ; has lain;
love lives a- gain , that with the dead has been :
love is come a - gain like wheat that springeth green .

2. In the grave they laid him, Love whom men had slain,
   thinking that never he would wake again,
   laid in the earth like grain that sleeps unseen:
   love is come again like wheat that springeth green.

3. Forth he came at Easter, like the risen grain,
   he that for three days in the grave had lain,
   quick from the dead my risen Lord is seen:
   love is come again like wheat that springeth green.

4. When our hearts are wintry, grieving or in pain,
   thy touch can call us back to life again,
   fields of our heart that dead and bare have been:
   love is come again like wheat that springeth green.

Words: J.M.C. Crum
Music: Traditional French Melody

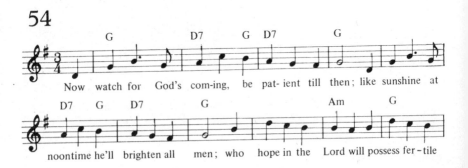

Now watch for God's com-ing, be pat- ient till then; like sunshine at
noontime he'll brighten all men; who hope in the Lord will possess fer – tile

land; the poor he will wel-come and grasp by the hand.

2. Man's steps are directed, God watches his path;
   he guides him and holds him and saves him from wrath,
   and though he may fall he will not go headlong,
   for God gives sound footing and keeps him from wrong.

3. So wait for his coming, be patient till then;
   the wicked are armed and would kill honest men.
   Their arms shall be broken, no refuge they'll see,
   but saved are the needy by God's own decree.

4. Now those who do evil will wither like grass,
   like green of the springtime they fade and they pass,
   so trust in the Lord and to him give your life,   *Words: Willard F. Jabusch*
   he'll bring heart's desires and peace in our strife.   *Music: Traditional Catalonian Carol*

55

Spi - rit of the li - ving God, fall a-fresh on me.

Spi - rit of the li - ving God, fall afresh on me.

Break me, melt me, mould me, fill me.

Spi - rit of the li - ving God, fall a- fresh on me.

Words and Music: Michael Iverson

56

He was born like you and I in a bo- dy which must die, yet his death was not for ev- er —— he lives on. Who is to this, like you and I who was born live and die, yet his death was not for ev- er —— he lives on?

Chorus
Deep, deep, deep, is the mys- te- ry I sing. Dark, dark, dark is the rid- dle. —— He was born like you and I in a bo- dy which must die, yet his death was not for ev - er: he lives on.

2. Not a soul, so it is said,
   saw him raised up from the dead,
   yet by now the story's known throughout the world.
   Who is this whom it is said
   no one saw raised from the dead,
   yet by now the story's known throughout the world?

3. His believers, when they've met,
   know he's there with them, and yet
   he's with God (what makes us think that's somewhere else?)
   Who is this who, when they've met,
   is right there with them, and yet
   he's with God (what makes us think that's somewhere else?)

Words and Music:
Hubert Richards

57

Here's a child for you, O Lord, we shall cher-ish,

we shall care. We'll be faith-ful to your Word,

for we want this child to share your love-light.

2. May he hold his head up high,
   graceful, joyful, strong of limb.
   May his eyes be clear and bright,
   seeing beauty in all things
   that you've made.

3. We were young ourselves, O Lord,
   we were eager, we were fresh
   like the opening buds of spring,
   and we wanted happiness
   in your way.

4. Then, at times, we went astray,
   we were foolish, we were weak,
   and the innocence we had
   vanished like the trace of feet
   when snow melts.

5. But we come, O Lord and king,
   at your bidding, and we pray
   that the precious gift we bring
   will grow stronger every day
   in your love.

6. By the water poured out here
   and our promise, we believe,
   he will master every fear,
   and at last will come to see
   your Godhead.

Words and Music: Estelle White

58

He's got the whole world —— in his hand. He's got the

whole world —— in his hand. He's got the whole wide world ——

in his hand. He's got the whole world in his hand.

2. He's got you and me, brother, in his hand. . .   4. He's got everybody here in his hand . . .

3. He's got you and me, sister, in his hand. . .   5. He's got the whole world in his hand. . .

Words and Music: Traditional

Go, the Mass is en- ded, chil-dren of the Lord.

Take his Word to oth- ers as you've heard it spo- ken to you.

Go, the Mass is en- ded, go and tell the world the

Lord is good, the Lord is kind, and he loves ev'- ry- one.

2. Go, the Mass is ended,
   take his love to all.
   Gladden all who meet you,
   fill their hearts with hope and courage.
   Go, the Mass is ended,
   fill the world with love,
   and give to all what you've received
   — the peace and joy of Christ.

3. Go, the Mass is ended,
   strengthened in the Lord,
   lighten ev'ry burden,
   spread the joy of Christ around you.
   Go, the Mass is ended,
   take his peace to all.
   This day is yours to change the world
   — to make God known and loved.

Words and Music: Sister Marie Lydia Pereira

If now my mind was still, emp-ty of self,
cleansed of de-sire and will, all my thought's wealth,
then, where no ear can reach, deep in my soul,
I'd know the liv-ing Word who makes me whole.

2. All my imaginings
cannot suffice,
and if my thoughts have wings
they carry pride.
But, where no eye can see,
deep in my soul,
his love can pierce the dark,
making me whole.

3. So, in my emptiness,
waiting until
I give my nothingness
to be fulfilled,
he, where no hand can touch,
deep in my soul,
pours out his love divine
and makes me whole.

Words and Music: Estelle White

61

Eb(D)   Bb7(A7)   Eb(D)   Eb7(D7)

1. All that I am, all that I do, all that I'll
2 All that I dream, all that I pray, all that I'll

Ab(G)   Eb(D)   Bb7 (A7)   Eb(D)   Bb7(A7)

ev - er have, I of-fer now to you. Take and sanc - ti -
ev er make, I give to you to - day.

Eb(D)   F7 (E7)

fy these gifts for your hon-our, Lord. Know - ing that I

Bb7 (A7)   Eb(D)

love and serve you is e-nough re - ward. All that I

Bb7 (A7)   Eb(D)   Eb7(D7)   Ab(G)

am, all that I do, all that I'll ev- er have I

Eb(D)   Bb7 (A7)   Eb(D)

of- fer now to you.

Words and Music: Sebastian Temple

62

Chorus G   C   Am   D

All the na-tions of the earth, praise the Lord who brings to birth the

G   C   Am   D   G   *fine*

great - est star, the small-est flower. Al- le- lu - ia.

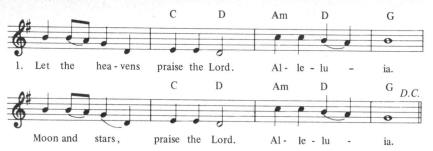

1. Let the hea-vens praise the Lord. Al-le-lu - ia.

Moon and stars, praise the Lord. Al-le-lu - ia.

2. Snow capped mountains, praise the Lord.
   Alleluia.
   Rolling hills, praise the Lord.
   Alleluia.

3. Deep sea water, praise the Lord.
   Alleluia.
   Gentle rain, praise the Lord.
   Alleluia.

4. Roaring lion, praise the Lord.
   Alleluia.
   Singing birds, praise the Lord.
   Alleluia.

5. Kings and princes, praise the Lord.
   Alleluia.
   Young and old, praise the Lord.
   Alleluia.

Words: Michael Cockett   Music: Kevin Mayhew

63

All this world be - longs to Je - sus, ev' - ry-thing is

his by right; all on the land, all in the sea;

ev' - ry - thing is his by right.

2. Shining stars in all their beauty
   are outnumbered by his gifts.
   Sand on the shore, stars in the sky,
   are outnumbered by his gifts.

3. Ev'ry foot that starts a-dancing
   taps a rhythm full of hope;
   full of his joy, full of his hope,
   taps a rhythm full of hope.

4. All that's good reflects his goodness;
   may it lead us back to him.
   All that is good, all that is true,
   may it lead us back to him.

5. So give thanks for what he's given;
   touch and taste, and feet to dance;
   eyes for the lights, ears for the sound,
   for the wonders of our Lord.

Music: Traditional Westerwald Melody   *Words: Willard F. Jabusch*

64

Ho-ly, ho- ly, ho- ly, ho- ly. Ho-ly

ho- ly, ho- ly Lord God al- migh – ty. And we

lift our hearts before you as a to-ken of our love. Ho- ly,

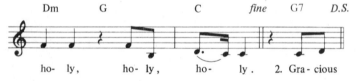

ho- ly, ho- ly, ho- ly . 2. Gra- cious

2. Gracious Father, gracious Father,
we are glad to be your children, gracious Father.
And we lift our heads before you as a token of our love,
gracious Father, gracious Father.

3. Precious Jesus, precious Jesus,
we are glad you have redeemed us, precious Jesus.
And we lift our hands before you as a token of our love,
precious Jesus, precious Jesus.

4. Holy Spirit, Holy Spirit,
come and fill our hearts anew, Holy Spirit.
And we lift our voice before you as a token of our love,
Holy Spirit, Holy Spirit.

5. Hallelujah, hallelujah,
hallelujah, hallelujah, hallelujah.
And we lift our hearts before you as a token of our love,
hallelujah, hallelujah.

Words and Music: Jimmy Owens

Am(Gm)   C(B♭)   D(C)

I won-der as I wan-der out un- der the sky, how

Am(Gm)   Dm(Cm)   Am(Gm)

Je- sus the Saviour did come for to die for poor ord'n'ry people like

F(E♭)   G(F)   Am(Gm)   D7(C7)   G7 (F7)   Dm(Cm)

you and like I. I won-der as I wander out un - der the sky.

2. When Mary birthed Jesus, 'twas in a cow's stall
   with wise men and farmers and shepherds and all.
   But high from God's heaven a star's light did fall,
   and the promise of ages it did then recall.

3. If Jesus had wanted for any wee thing,
   a star in the sky, or a bird on the wing,
   or all of God's angels in heav'n for to sing,
   he surely could have it, 'cause he was the king.

Words and Music: Traditional

66

At the name of Je - sus ev' - ry knee shall bow,
ev' - ry tongue con- fess him King of Glo- ry now.
'Tis the Fa-ther's plea-sure we should call him Lord,
who from the be- gin - ning was the migh - ty Lord.

2. At his voice creation
   sprang at once to sight,
   all the angel faces,
   all the hosts of light,
   thrones and dominations,
   stars upon their way,
   all the heav'nly orders
   in their great array.

3. Humbled for a season
   to receive a name
   from the lips of sinners
   unto whom he came,
   faithfully he bore it
   spotless to the last,
   brought it back victorious
   when from death he passed.

4. Bore it up triumphant
   with its human light
   through all ranks of creatures
   to the central height,
   to the throne of Godhead,
   to the Father's breast,
   filled it with the glory
   of that perfect rest.

5. Name him, brothers, name him
   with love as strong as death,
   but with awe and wonder
   and with bated breath.
   He is God the Saviour,
   he is Christ the Lord,
   ever to be worshipped,
   trusted and adored.

Words: Caroline Maria Noel   *Music: Michael Brierley*

67

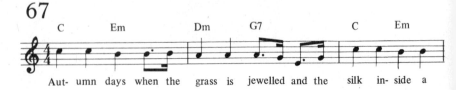

Aut- umn days when the grass is jewelled and the silk in- side a

chestnut shell, jet planes meeting in the air to get re-fuelled, all these things I love so well. So I mustn't for-get. No, I mustn't for-get, to say a great big thank-you, I mustn't for-get.

2. Clouds that look like familiar faces, and a
   winter's moon with frosted rings,
   smell of bacon as I fasten up my laces,
   and the song the milkman sings.

3. Whipped up spray that is rainbow-scattered, and a
   swallow curving in the sky.
   Shoes so comfy though they're worn-out and they're battered,
   and the taste of apple-pie.

4. Scent of gardens when the rain's been falling, and a
   minnow darting down a stream,
   picked-up engine that's been stuttering and stalling,
   and a win for my home team.

Words and Music: Estelle White

68

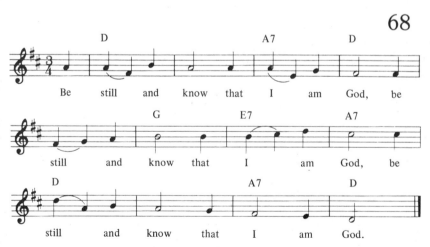

Be still and know that I am God, be still and know that I am God, be still and know that I am God.

2. I am the Lord that healeth thee. . .   3. In thee, O Lord, I put my trust. . .

Words and Music: Anonymous

69

If like old King Sol - o - mon, the Lord gave me the task of find - ing what I want from him, for these three gifts I'll ask. I'll ask for faith, hope and char - i - ty to strengthen me! Faith, hope and char - i - ty to set me free! Faith, hope and char - i - ty to lead me where I meet my Sav - iour in dai - ly prayer.

2. Faith will always lead me to
   the things that are unseen,
   while hope will spur my fainting heart
   to hold the Christian dream.

3. Love surpasses knowledge and
   is strength when we are weak;
   for God is love, and love is God,
   the honey all men seek.

4. Faith and hope may pass away,
   but love will always be,
   and bind all men together,
   into one big family.

Words and Music: Sebastian Temple

As bread my Lord comes to me, though I

am un - wor - thy. He heals me, bo - dy and soul,

and sets my spi - rit free. For he is my

Sa - viour and my God, yes, he is my Sa - viour and my God.

2. I am far nearer to him
than the air I breathe.
With joy I welcome him home,
he satisfies my heart's need.
For he is my Saviour and my God,
yes, he is my Saviour and my God.

3. The still, small voice that I hear
always is reminding
my soul of love and of peace
that passeth understanding.
For he is my Saviour and my God,
yes, he is my Saviour and my God.

Words and Music: Estelle White

I saw the grass, I saw the trees and the boats a-long the shore. I saw the shapes of ma-ny things I had on-ly sensed be-fore. And I saw the fa-ces of men more clear-ly than if I had nev-er been blind, the lines of en-vy a-round their lips and the greed and the hate in their eyes. And I turned a-way, yes, I turned a-way, for I had seen the per-fect face of a real and pro-per man, the man who brought me from the dark in-to light, where life be-gan.

2. I hurried then away from town
   to a quiet, lonely place.
   I found a clear, unruffled pool
   and I gazed upon my face.
   And I saw the image of me more clearly
   than if I had never been blind,
   the lines of envy around the lips
   and the greed and the hate in the eyes.
   And I turned away, yes, I turned away,
   for I had seen the perfect face of a real
       and proper man,
   the man who'd brought me from the
   dark into light, where life began.

   Words and Music: Estelle White

3. I made my way into the town,
   to the busy, crowded streets,
   the shops and stalls and alley-ways,
   to the squalor and the heat.
   And I saw the faces of men more clearly
   than if I had never been blind,
   the lines of sorrow around their lips
   and the child looking out from their eyes,
   and I turned to them, yes, I turned to
       them,
   remembering the perfect face of a real
       and proper man,
   the man who'd brought me from the dark
   into light, where life began.

72

2. I will sing your praises. . .

3. I will give you honour. . .

For an effective second part in this song sing a third above the tune (starting on B)

Words and Music: Malcolm Campbell-Carr

73

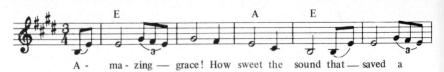

A - ma - zing — grace! How sweet the sound that — saved a

wretch like me. I once was lost but now I'm found was

blind, but now I see.

2. 'Twas grace that taught my heart to fear,
   and grace my fears relieved.
   How precious did that grace appear
   the hour I first believed.

3. Through many dangers, toils and snares
   I have already come.
   'Tis grace hath brought me safe thus far,
   and grace will lead me home.

4. The Lord has promised good to me;
   his word my hope secures.
   He will my shield and portion be
   as long as life endures.

   Words: John Newton
   Music: Traditional American Melody

74

A — men, a - men, a - men, a- men, a - men.

Music: Negro Spiritual

All cre-a-tion, bless the Lord. Earth and hea-ven, bless the Lord.

Spi-rits, pow-ers, bless the Lord. Praise him for - ev - er.

Sun and moon, praise the Lord. Stars and plan-ets, bless the Lord.

Dews and showers, bless the Lord. Praise him for — ev— er.

2. Winds and breezes, bless the Lord.
   Spring and Autumn, bless the Lord.
   Winter, Summer, bless the Lord.
   Praise him for ever.
   Fire and heat, bless the Lord.
   Frost and cold, bless the Lord.
   Ice and snow, bless the Lord.
   Praise him forever.

3. Night and daytime, bless the Lord.
   Light and darkness, bless the Lord.
   Clouds and lightning, bless the Lord.
   Praise him forever.
   All the earth, bless the Lord.
   Hills and mountains, bless the Lord.
   Trees and flowers, bless the Lord.
   Praise him forever.

4. Springs and rivers, bless the Lord.
   Seas and oceans, bless the Lord.
   Whales and fishes, bless the Lord.
   Praise him forever.
   Birds and insects, bless the Lord.
   Beasts and cattle, bless the Lord.
   Let all creatures bless the Lord.
   Praise him forever.

5. Let God's people bless the Lord.
   Men and women, bless the Lord.
   All creation, bless the Lord.
   Praise him forever.
   Let God's people bless the Lord.
   Men and women, bless the Lord.
   All creation, bless the Lord.
   Praise him forever.

Words and Music: Hayward Osborne

Chorus

Praise the Lord, and sing hal- le- lu- jah, hal- le- lu- jah, hal- le- lu- jah. Praise the Lord, and sing hal- le- lu- jah, hal- le- lu- jah, hal- le- lu- jah.

fine

1. Praise him for the sun and for the stars a bove, hal- le- lu- jah, hal- le- lu- jah. Praise him with your broth- ers for he is the God of love, hal- le- lu- jah, hal- le- lu- jah.

DC

2. Praise him when you're happy,
   praise him when you're sad,
   hallelujah, hallelujah.
   He's the God who saves us
   and his message makes us glad
   hallelujah, hallelujah.

3. Praise him in the morning,
   praise him in the night,
   hallelujah, hallelujah.
   Praise him in the thunder
   for he is the God of might,
   hallelujah, hallelujah.

Words and Music: Gerald O'Mahony.

This song may be sung as a round (the second voice enters at the double bar).

77

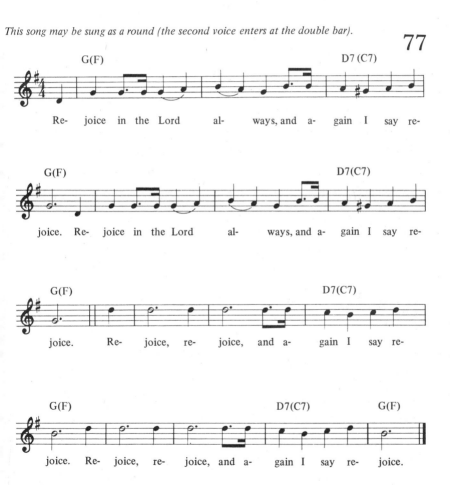

Re- joice in the Lord al- ways, and a- gain I say re-

joice. Re- joice in the Lord al- ways, and a- gain I say re-

joice. Re- joice, re- joice, and a- gain I say re-

joice. Re- joice, re- joice, and a- gain I say re- joice.

Words and Music: Anonymous

1. Oh, the Lord looked down from his window in the sky, said:
"I cre-a-ted man but I can't re-mem-ber why!
No-thing but figh-ting since cre-a-tion day. I'll
send a lit-tle wa-ter and wash them all a-way". Oh, the
Lord came down and looked a-round a spell.
There was Mi-ster Noah be — ha — ving mighty well. And
that is the rea-son the Scrip-tures re-cord
No-ah found grace in the eyes of the Lord.

E(F)

Chorus

B7(C)

Noah found grace in the eyes of the Lord, Noah found grace in the

E(F)

A(B♭)

eyes of the Lord, Noah found grace in the eyes of the Lord and he

E(F)   B7(C)   E(F)

left him high and dry.

2. The Lord said: "Noah, there's going to be a flood,
   there's going to be some water, there's going to be some mud,
   so take off your hat, Noah, take off your coat,
   get Sham, Ham and Japhat and build yourself a boat".
   Noah said: "Lord, I don't believe I could".
   The Lord said: "Noah, get yourself some wood.
   You never know what you can do till you try.
   Build it fifty cubits wide and thirty cubits high".

3. Noah said: "There she is, there she is, Lord!"
   The Lord said: "Noah, it's time to get aboard.
   Take of each creature a he and a she
   and of course take Mrs.Noah and the whole family".
   Noah said: "Lord, it's getting mighty dark".
   The Lord said: "Noah, get those creatures in the ark".
   Noah said: "Lord, it's beginning to pour".
   The Lord said: "Noah, hurry up and close the door".

4. The ark rose up on the bosom of the deep.
   After forty days Mr.Noah took a peep.
   He said: "We're not moving, Lord, where are we at?"
   The Lord said: "You're sitting right on Mount Ararat".
   Noah said: "Lord, it's getting nice and dry".
   The Lord said: "Noah, see my rainbow in the sky.
   Take all your creatures and people the earth
   and be sure that you're not more trouble than you're worth".

Words and Music: Traditional

I love the warmth of the sun, the dancing light in a stream, and yet in win-ter it seems that sum-mer days were a dream. But one day there'll be no more goodbyes, no grieving, no more sighs, tears will be gent-ly wiped a-way, and as we now see as in a glass, things will be clear at last, all beauty will be here to stay.

2. I love the look of a child,
   the joy of life in his face.
   But as I watch him I know
   that glow of childhood must fade.

3. I love the sound of the sea,
   the rise and fall of the waves.
   But as the tide brings men home
   it also takes them away.

4. I love those hours of delight
   that I have spent with my friends.
   But there's a time of farewell,
   for every party must end.

Words and Music: Estelle White

Chorus

A - lone with on -ly you, my God I journey on my way. What need I fear when you are near, O King of night and day?

1. I am the way, the sign-post for your journey. You'll need no gold nor sil - ver in your belt, no bag, no shoes, no staff to ease your load. I am your guide and one day I'll say to you: "This is your journey's end. Come with me, my good and faith- ful friend".

2.

I am the Truth, the password for your journey.
Stand tall and shout for all the world to hear
that Christ our Lord has come to save all men.
I am your guide and one day I'll say to you:
"This is your journey's end.
Come with me, my good and faithful friend."

3.

I am the Life, the purpose of your journey.
This world is but a shadow of the next,
a passing cloud against th 'eternal sun.
I am your guide and one day I'll say to you:
"This is your journey's end.
Come with me, my good and faithful friend."

Words and Music: Kevin Mayhew

81

Oh, the love of my Lord is the es-sence of all that I love here on earth. All the beau-ty I see he has giv-en to me and his giv-ing is gen-tle as si-lence.

2. Every day, every hour, every moment
   have been blessed by the strength of his love.
   At the turn of each tide
   he is there at my side,
   and his touch is as gentle as silence.

3. There've been times when I've turned from his presence,
   and I've walked other paths, other ways.
   But I've called on his name
   in the dark of my shame,
   and his mercy was gentle as silence.

Words and Music: Estelle White

82

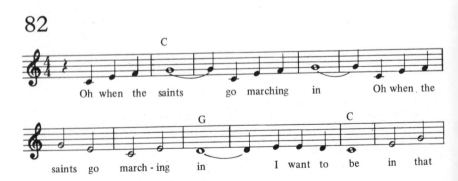

Oh when the saints go marching in Oh when the saints go march-ing in I want to be in that

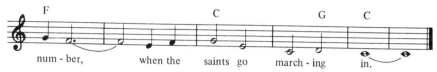

num - ber,　　when the　saints go　march - ing　in.

2. Oh when the drums begins to bang. . .

3. Oh when the stars fall from the sky. . .

4. Oh when the moon turns into blood. . .

5. Oh when the sun turns into fire. . .

6. Oh when the fires begin to blaze. . .

7. Oh when the Lord calls out the names. . .

Words and Music: Traditional

83

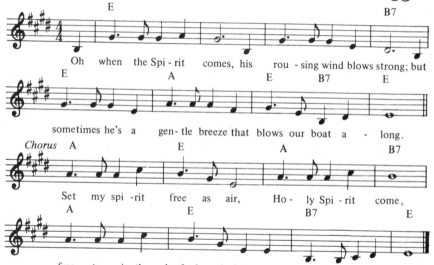

Oh when the Spi - rit comes, his rou - sing wind blows strong; but

sometimes he's a gen - tle breeze that blows our boat a - long.

Chorus

Set my spi - rit free as air, Ho - ly Spi - rit come,

free to praise through foul and fair, un - til your will be done.

2. God's Spirit comes as fire,
   to burn away our sins,
   but his is too the gentle warmth
   that warms the cold within.

3. Sometimes his waters roar
   to drown away our fear,
   but he can bathe the troubled brow
   with cooling waters clear.

4. The Spirit comes in power,
   to break a prison wall,
   but his is, too, the gentle strength
   that causes tears to fall.

5. O Holy Spirit free
   like water, wind and fire,
   come with your many varied gifts
   to fill our hearts desire.

Words and Music: Gillian Simpson

I watch the sun-rise light-ing the sky, cast-ing its sha-dows near. And on this morn-ing bright though it be, I feel those sha-dows near me.

Chorus

But you are al-ways close to me fol-low-ing all my ways. May I be al-ways close to you fol-low-ing all your ways, Lord.

2. I watch the sunlight
   shine through the clouds,
   warming the earth below.
   And at the mid-day
   life seems to say:
   "I feel your brightness near me."
   For you are always. . .

3. I watch the sunset
   fading away,
   lighting the clouds with sleep.
   And as the evening
   closes its eyes
   I feel your presence near me.
   For you are always. . .

4. I watch the moonlight
   guarding the night,
   waiting till morning comes.
   The air is silent,
   earth is at rest —
   only your peace is near me.
   Yes, you are always. . .

Words: John Glynn
Music: Colin Murphy

God be with you'til we meet a-gain! By his coun-sels guide, up-hold you,

with his sheep se-curely fold you; God be with you til we meet a-gain!

Chorus
'Til we meet! 'til we meet! 'til we meet at Je - sus' feet;

'til we meet! 'til we meet! God be with you'til we meet a - gain!

2. God be with you 'til we meet again!
   Neath his wings securely hide you,
   daily manna still provide you;
   God be with you 'til we meet again!

3. God be with you 'til we meet again!
   Keep love's banner floating o'er you,
   smite death's threat'ning wave before you;
   God be with you 'til we meet again!

Words: Jeremiah Rankin
Music: William Tomer

Hap-py the man who wan-ders with the Lord. Hap-py the

man who knows how to live. Hap-py the man who

nev-er seeks re - ward, giv-ing be - cause he loves to give.

He seeks no gold, he wants no gain. He knows those

things are all in vain. He needs no praise nor hon-our.

too. His on-ly mot-to: "To your own self be true."

Hap-py the man who learned how to pray.

Happy the man who has a burn-ing goal. Hap-py the

man whose ser- vice needs no pay. This man has

found his own soul. ———— Happy the man, hap-py the

man of the Lord.

Words and Music: Sebastian Temple

87

I be-lieve in God al-migh-ty, who made heav'n and earth.
I be-lieve in one Lord, Je-sus Christ, his on-ly Son.
God from God and Light from Light, the one true God a-bove,
with the Fa-ther he is one, cre-a-tor of all things. Oh
I be-lieve in God al-migh-ty, who made heav'n and
earth. Yes, I be-lieve in God al-migh-ty,
who made heav'n and earth.

2. For us all he came to earth and lived as one of us.
   For our sake he suffered death. They nailed him to a cross.
   But no earthly grave could hold the Lord of heav'n and earth;
   bursting forth he rose again, just as the prophets said.

3. Forty days he walked the earth, a dead man come alive.
   Then he bids his friends farewell, returning to his heav'n.
   He will come again to judge the living and the dead.
   He is Lord of all the worlds; his kingdom has no end.

4. I believe in God the Father, Spirit and the Son.
I believe the Church is holy, universal, one.
And through water all our guilt is cleansed — we are made new.
Dying we will rise again to live for ever more.

Words and Music:
Kevin Mayhew

88

I have counted the cost of the years that are gone, all the bat-tles I lost and the few that I won. And the plans that would dawn that I somewhere mis-laid, and the hopes that were born, and the dreams that decayed. Still in spite of the loss and the labour in vain, still in spite of it all, I'll start ov-er a - gain, still in spite of it all I'll start ov-er a - gain.

2. Lord, I thought that I knew
all the questions you'd ask,
what you'd want me to do,
ev'ry truth, ev'ry task;
and your word seemed so near,
and your light seemed so strong,
and the road seemed so clear
that you called me along.
Still, in spite of the hopes
time has carried away,
still in spite of it all
I will walk in your way,
still, in spite of it all,
I will walk in your way.

3. I had mastered it all,
all my answers were true,
but when I heard your call
all your questions were new;
all the ways that you came,
the disguises you wore,
you were just not the same,
not the same anymore.
Still in spite of the loss
and in spite of the pain,
still in spite of it all,
I will find you again,
still in spite of it all,
I will find you again.

Words and Music:
Kevin Nichols

On a hill far a—way stood an old rug—ged cross, the
emb-lem of suff'-ring and shame; and I loved that old cross where the
dear-est and best for a world of lost sinners was slain. So I'll
cher-ish the old rug-ged cross, till my tro-phies at last I lay
down; I will cling to the old rug-ged cross and ex-
change it some-day for a crown.

2. Oh that old rugged cross, so despised by the world,
   has a wondrous attraction for me:
   for the dear Lamb of God left his glory above
   to bear it to dark Calvary.

3. In the old rugged cross, stained with blood so divine,
   a wondrous beauty I see.
   For 'twas on that old cross Jesus suffered and died
   to pardon and sanctify me.

4. To the old rugged cross I will ever be true,
   its shame and reproach gladly bear.
   Then he'll call me some day to my home far away
   there his glory for ever I'll share.

Words and Music: George Bennar

Holy Spirit of fire flame ev-er-las-ting, so bright and clear, speak this day in our hearts.. Light-en our dark-ness and purge us of fear, Ho-ly Spi-rit of fire. The wind can blow or be still, or wa-ter be parched by the sun. A fire can die in-to dust: but here the e-ter-nal Spi-rit of God tells us a new world's be-gun.

2. Holy Spirit of love,
    strong are the faithful who trust your pow'r.
    Love who conquers our will,
    teach us the words of the gospel of peace,
    Holy Spirit of love.

3. Holy Spirit of God,
    flame everlasting so bright and clear,
    speak this day in our hearts.
    Lighten our darkness and purge us of fear,
    Holy Spirit of God.

Words and Music: John Glynn

91

Chorus Em / D / Em / C / D / Em

On we go to Je - ru - sa - lem, the ci - ty of the house of God,

D / Em / C / D / Em *fine*

pil - grim peo - ple, we seek the Lord, the Lord of the house of rock.

C / B7 / Em

1. Age on age pro — claims his prais - es each declares him Lord of all.

B / B7 *D.C.*

Count-less mil - lions sing his glo - ry, answer-ing his pil - grim call.

2. Peace he promised to our fathers
in the ancient desert-land;
peace he offers in abundance
to his faithful pilgrim-band.

3. All we have is offered to him
as we come to sing his praise.
Blessed is the Lord of heaven,
mighty God of all our days.

Words and Music: Kevin Mayhew

92

Em A / D G / Em / C / D / G

One, one, e - ter - nal one, the Fa - ther be-fore cre - a - tion was be-gun.

Em A / D G / Em / C / B7 / E

One, one, e - ter - nal one, the Fa - ther of God his ve - ry dear Son.

Chorus A / E / B7 / E

God is love, he who dwells in love dwells in God and God in him.

2. Two, two, eternal two,
   the word of the Father only Jesus knew.
   Two, two, eternal two,
   just living the love he knew to be true.

3. Three, three, eternal three,
   the Spirit of love before man came to be.
   Three, three, eternal three,
   a fire we can feel but never can see.

4. Praise, praise the Trinity,
   where joy, love and truth are one simplicity.
   Praise, praise the Trinity,
   whose life is to love, and ever must be.

Words: Damian Webb
Music: André Popp

93

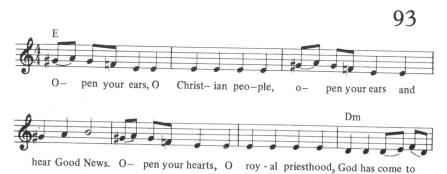

O— pen your ears, O Christ— ian peo—ple, o— pen your ears and

hear Good News. O— pen your hearts, O roy - al priesthood, God has come to

Chorus

you. God has spo- ken to his peo- ple, al — le — lu — ia.

And his words are words of wis—dom, al — le — lu — ia.

2. Israel comes to greet the Saviour,
   Judah is glad to see his day.
   From East and West the peoples travel,
   He will show the way.

3. He who has ears to hear his message:
   he who has ears, then let him hear.
   He who would learn the way of wisdom,
   let him hear God's words.

Words: W.F. Jabusch
Music: Israeli Folk Song

94

Do you want my hands, Lord? Do you want my hands, Lord? Do you want my hands, Lord, all through the day, to help the needy and the sick and the poor, to work from morn till the day is o'er? I give you my hands, I give you my hands, I give you my hands to- day.

2. Do you want my feet, Lord? (2)
   Do you want my feet, Lord, all through the day,
   to go each day to those who need a friend,
   to walk with the lonely till their journey's end?
   I give you my feet. (2)
   I give you my feet today.

3. Do you want my voice, Lord? (2)
   Do you want my voice, Lord, all through the day,
   to speak to all who need your words of love,
   to tell of our Father and our home above?
   I give you my voice (2)
   I give you my voice today.

4. Do you want my heart, Lord? (2)
   Do you want my heart, Lord, all through the day,
   to love ev'rybody leaving nobody out,
   to give your love to those in pain and doubt?
   I give you my heart. (2)
   I give you my heart today.

Words and Music: Sister M. Pereira

95

Do - na no - bis pa - cem, pac-em. Do - na no - bis

pa cem. Do - na no - bis pa - cem.

Do - na no - bis pa - cem. Do - na

no - bis pa - cem. Do - na no-bis pa - cem.

Words and Music: Anonymous

Dust, dust, and ash - es lie ov - er on my grave. Dust, dust and

ash - es lie ov - er on my grave. Dust, dust and ash- es lie

ov - er on my grave, and the Lord shall bear my spi - rit

home, and the Lord shall — bear my spi - rit home.

2. They crucified my saviour, and nailed him to the cross. . .

3. And Mary came a-running, her saviour for to see. . .

4. The angels said: "He's not here, he's gone to Galilee". . .

5. He rose, he rose, he rose up, he rose up from the dead. . .   *Words and Music: Traditional*

97

Fa-ther, in hea-ven, from your great good-ness we place be-

fore you this bread and wine. Pour forth your Spi-rit on your cre-

a-tion and of your dear Son make them the sign.

2. Breathe on our gifts here
which human hands made,
speak words of power,
your words of might.
May they be for us
your Son in glory,
may they make present
the world's true light.

3. May we with him be one in him
one in his passion,
one in his dying,
one in his strife.
Father, we offer
ourselves in union
one with each other
sharing his life.

Words: Michael Evans
Music: Malcolm Campbell-Carr.

98

For from him, and through him, and to him are all

things; to God be the glo-ry for ev-er. A-

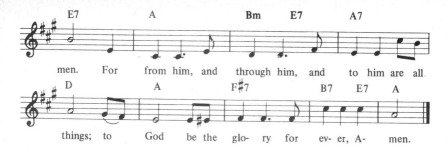

men. For from him, and through him, and to him are all.

things; to God be the glo- ry for ev- er, A- men.

Words and Music: Ena Thompson

99

From the field and from the ci- ty, call the peo- ples of the earth

for the buil- ding of the kingdom; tell them of its birth.

2. Hew the wood and draw the water,
   build the city stone by stone,
   Christ will be our master builder,
   no one builds alone.

3. Summon labourers, summon wise men,
   skilful hand and loving heart,
   there's a place for every talent,
   each can play its part.

4. Love the Lord and love your neighbour,
   that is God's own master-plan,
   in this kingdom there's no hatred,
   man's at peace with man.

5. In this kingdom there'll be dancing,
   singing and a lordly feast,
   every creature finds a home there,
   greatest to the least.

6. Let us start to build the city,
   with the power of God's own love,
   walls that rise from earth's foundation
   to the heav'n above.

Words and Music: John Harriott

100

Chorus

Day by day in the mar-ket place I play my flute all day. I have piped to them all, but no- bo- dy dan -ces.

Day by day in the mar-ket place I play my flute all day, and who- ev- er you be, won't you dance with me.

1. At Ca - na, when my mo-ther plead- ed that they were short of wine, I gave them all the wine they need - ed ; their hap - pi- ness was mine.

2. Once, when I found poor Peter quaking,
   I let him walk the sea.
   I filled their fishing nets to breaking
   that day in Galilee.

3. While all the world despised the sinner
   I showed him hope again,
   and gave the honours at that dinner
   to Mary Magdalene.

4. Lazarus from the tomb advancing
   once more drew life's sweet breath.
   You too will leave the churchyard dancing,
   for I have conquered death.

Words and Music: Aimé Duval

On this house your bles-sing, Lord. On this house your grace bestow. On this house your bles-sing, Lord. May it come and nev-er
go. Bringing peace and joy and hap-pi-ness, bringing
love that knows no end. On this house your blessing
Lord. On this house your bles-ing send.

2. On this house your loving, Lord.
   May it overflow each day.
   On this house your loving, Lord.
   May it come and with us stay.
   Drawing us in love and unity
   by the love received from you.
   On this house your loving, Lord.
   May it come each day anew.

4. On this house your calling, Lord.
   May it come to us each day.
   On this house your calling, Lord.
   May it come to lead the way.
   Filling us with nobler yearnings, Lord,
   calling us to live in you.
   On this house your calling, Lord.
   May it come each day anew.

3. On this house your giving, Lord.
   May it turn and ever flow.
   On this house your giving, Lord.
   On this house your wealth bestow.
   Filling all our hopes and wishes, Lord,
   in the way you know is best.
   On this house your giving, Lord.
   May it come and with us rest.

Words and Music: Sister M. Pereira

102

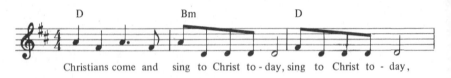

Christians come and sing to Christ to-day, sing to Christ to - day,

sing to Christ to - day, ga - ther in his house to - day.

2. Christians come, and pray to Christ today . . .

3. Christians come, and trust in Christ today . . .

4. Christians come, and learn from Christ today . . .

5. Christians come, and work for Christ today . . .

6. Christians come, and walk with Christ today . . .

7. Christians come, and live with Christ today . . .   *Words and Music: from Ghana*

Chorus

I sing a song to you, Lord, a song of love and praise. All glo-ry be to you, Lord, through ev-er-las-ting days. 1. Ho-ly, ho-ly, ho-ly, migh-ty Lord and God. He who was and is now, and who is to come.

2. Worthy is the slain Lamb,
   honour him and praise.
   We rejoice with gladness,
   sing our love today.

3. He has used his power,
   has begun his reign.
   So rejoice, you heavens,
   and proclaim his name.

4. Shine your light on us, Lord,
   let us know your way.
   Be our guide for ever,
   make us yours today.

Words and Music: Richard Beaumont

104

Gath-er peo-ples of the earth, thank the Lord for all his deeds,
open-ing up the life of hea-ven, ans-w'ring all our earth-ly needs.

2. Thank him for the burning sun,
   thank him for the cooling rain,
   thank him for the hours of ease,
   thank him for the flower of pain.

3. Thank him for the seed of hope,
   thank him for the flame of love,
   thank him for the olive branch
   carried by the peaceful dove.

4. Thank him for the cheerful day,
   thank him for the nights of woe,
   heat and pleasure, cold and pain,
   all through which we learn and grow.

5. Thank him for this Sacrament,
   feeding us with life divine,
   humble God in humble guise,
   Word made flesh through bread and wine.

6. Praise the Father and the Son,
   praise the Spirit of them given,
   living in us here on earth,
   calling us to highest heaven.

Words: John Harriott
Music: Malcolm Campbell-Carr

105

Give me joy in my heart, keep me prais-ing'. Give me

joy in my heart I pray. Give me joy in my heart, keep me
prais-ing. Keep me prais-ing 'till the end of day. Sing ho-san-na!

Sing ho- san- na! Sing ho- san- na to the King of Kings!

Sing ho- san- na! Sing ho- san- na! Sing ho-san- na to the King!

2. Give me peace in my heart, keep me resting. . .

3. Give me love in my heart, keep me serving. . .

Words and Music: Traditional

106

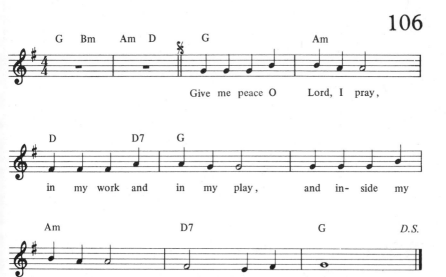

Give me peace O Lord, I pray,

in my work and in my play, and in- side my

heart and mind, Lord, give me peace.

2. Give peace to the world, I pray,
   let all quarrels cease today.
   May we spread your light and love.
   Lord, give us peace.

Words and Music: Estelle White

107

Love is his word, love is his way feasting with men, fast-ing a-lone,
liv-ing and dy-ing, ri-sing a-gain. Love, on-ly love is his way.

Chorus

Rich-er than gold is the love of my Lord, bet-ter than splen dour and wealth.

2. Love is his way, love is his mark,
sharing his last Passover feast,
Christ at the table, host to the Twelve.
Love, only love, is his mark.

3. Love is his mark, love is his sign,
bread for our strength, wine for our joy,
"This is my body, this is my blood ",
Love, only love, is his sign.

4. Love is his sign, love is his news.
"Do this," he said, "lest you forget
all my deep sorrow, all my dear blood ",
Love, only love, is his news.

5. Love is his news, love is his name.
we are his own, chosen and called,
family, brethren, cousins and kin.
Love, only love, is his name.

6. Love is his name, love is his law.
Hear his command, all who are his:
"Love one another, I have loved you ",
Love, only love, is his law.

7. Love is his law, love is his word:
love of the Lord, Father and Word,
love of the Spirit, God ever one.
Love, only love, is his word.

Words: Luke Connaughton   *Music: Anthony Milner*

108

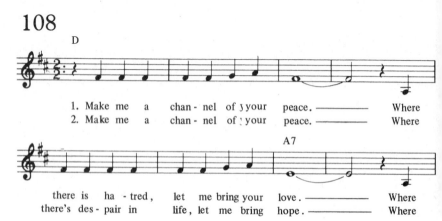

1. Make me a chan-nel of your peace. ———— Where
2. Make me a chan-nel of your peace. ———— Where

there is ha-tred, let me bring your love. ———— Where
there's des-pair in life, let me bring hope. ———— Where

there is in-ju-ry, your par-don, Lord. ——— And
there is dark-ness ——— on-ly light. ——— And

where there's doubt, true faith in you. ———
where there's sad-ness ev - er joy. ———

Oh, Mas-ter, grant that I may nev-er seek ——— so

much to be con-soled as to con-sole, ——— to be

un-der-stood as to un-der-stand, ——— to be

loved, as to love, with all my soul. ———

3. Make me a chan-nel of your peace. ——— It

is in par-don-ing that we are par-doned, ——— in

giv-ing to all men that we re-ceive, ——— and in

dy-ing that we're born to e-ter-nal life.

Words and Music:
Sebastian Temple

109

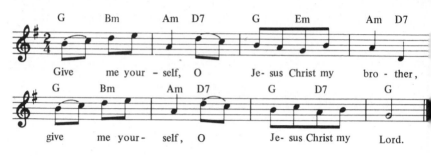

G　　Bm　　Am　D7　　　G　　Em　　　Am　D7

Give　me your – self,　O　Je- sus Christ my　bro - ther,

G　　Bm　　Am　D7　　　G　　D7　　　G

give　me your- self,　O　Je- sus Christ my　Lord.

2. Give me your peace, O Jesus Christ my brother,
   Give me your peace, O Jesus Christ my Lord.

3. Give me your love, O Jesus Christ my brother,
   Give me your love, O Jesus Christ my Lord.

4. Give me your heart, O Jesus Christ my brother,
   Give me your heart, O Jesus Christ my Lord.　　*Words and Music: Estelle White*

110

B♭(A)　　　　E♭(D)　　　　B♭(A)

Glo　ri - ous God,　King of cre - a - tion,　we

E♭(D)　　　B♭(A)　　　E♭(D)　　E7 (E7) B♭(A)

praise you　we　bless you, we　wor ship you in　song. Glo - ri - ous God,

E♭(D)　　　B♭(A)　　　　　　　F7 (E7)

in ad - o - ra - tion,　at your　feet we be -

B♭(A)　　　*fine*　F7 (E7)　　　　　　　B♭(A)

long.　Lord　of life,　Father al - migh - ty,

Lord of hearts, Christ the King. Lord of love,

Ho - ly Spi - rit, to whom we hom - age bring.

2. Glorious God, magnificent, holy,
   we love you, adore you, and come to you in pray'r.
   Glorious God, mighty, eternal,
   we sing your praise ev'rywhere.

Words and Music: Sebastian Temple

111

Chorus

Glo - ry, glo - ry, glo - ry to God in the high - est, and

peace to his peo - ple on earth. Our Lord and God and King of the

hea - vens, migh- ty God and Fa - ther, we wor-ship and give

thanks to you; we praise you for your glo - ry.

2. Lord Jesus Christ, the Son of the Father,
   Lamb of God, have mercy.
   You free the world from sinfulness,
   have mercy, Lord, have mercy.

3. Receive our prayer, O Son of the Father,
   hear our cry for mercy.
   As from your seat at his right hand
   you share the throne of glory.

4. For you are Lord, the One and the Holy.
   With the Holy Spirit
   you are the only Lord Most High,
   in glory with the Father.

Words: Michael Cockett
Music: Malcolm Campbell-Carr

112

In the earth the small seed is hidden and lies un- seen un-til it is bidden by springtime stir - rings up to the sunlight and sum-mer ripe-ning. Gol- den is the har - vest and precious the bread that you are, and give to us, Lord.

2.
In the vineyard branches are cut away
so that fresh young shoots may, with ev'ry day,
bend beneath the fruit as it ripens and
fills with promise.
Golden is the harvest and precious the
wine that you are,
and give to us, Lord.

3.
In me, Oh my Lord, plant the seed of love
nourished by your body and by your blood.
May my soul take wings and rise upwards to
new awakenings!
Golden is the light of your Godhead that
by love you have,
and give to us, Lord.

Words and Music: Estelle White

113

It's me, it's me, it's me, O Lord, stan - din' in the need of pray'r. It's

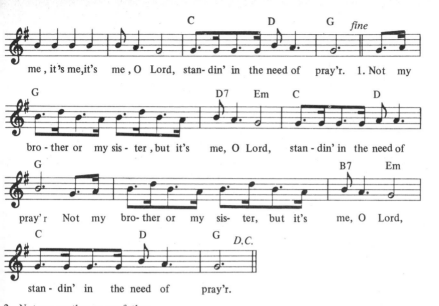

me , it's me,it's me , O Lord, stan- din' in the need of pray'r. 1. Not my

bro - ther or my sis - ter , but it's me, O Lord, stan - din' in the need of

pray' r Not my bro- ther or my sis - ter, but it's me, O Lord,

stan - din' in the need of pray'r.

2. Not my mother or my father...

3. Not the stranger or my neighbour...   *Words and Music: Negro Spiritual*

114

Just a clo- ser walk with thee, grant it, Je- sus if you please;

dai - ly walk- ing close to thee, let it be, dear Lord, let it be.

2. Through the day of toil that's near,
   if I fall, dear Lord, who cares.
   Who with me my burden share?
   None but thee, dear Lord, none but thee.

3. When my feeble life is o'er,
   time for me will be no more.
   Guide me gently, safely on
   to the shore, dear Lord, to the shore.

Words and Music: Traditional

115

G		C	G		'C		G	D7

Our Fa-ther who art in hea-ven, hal-lowed be thy name. Thy

G		C	G	G7	C		G

kingdom come, thy will be done on earth as *it* is in hea-ven. Give

Em		Am		D	D7	G

us this day our dai-ly bread and for - give us our trespass-ses, as

Em		Am	D	G	C

we forgive those who tres-pass a-gainst us. And lead us not in-to temp-

G	G7	C	G

ta—tion, but de— liv— er us from ev— il.   *Music: Estelle White*

116

G	Em	C	D7	G

Out and a — way

Em		C	D7	G

the mountains are cal— ling! Voi— ces are

Em	D7	G

clear and wide as the sky! Where is the

mus—ic I hear in my heart: soars ov— er val—leys as

swift as a lark; ech—oes the joy that has scattered the

Last time

dark; I am free.

2. Hear the wind sigh through leaves that are falling;
   see the wind sway the trees that are dry.
   Silent the darkness where thunder-clouds form;
   still is the world as it waits for the storm:
   now comes the lightning that heralds the dawn of the rain.

3. Water is clear, as clear as the moonlight;
   dew on the ground, a tear in the eye.
   Rivers and torrents have vanished before;
   oceans have coastlines and continents shores:
   boundless the flow that's unlocking the doors of my heart.

4. Free as the day my spirit is flying;
   eagles have wings, but none strong as these!
   Where have I found it, this life newly-grown?
   Gently, my heart says it's not of my own:
   deeper beyond me the Spirit has blown — he is love.

Words and Music: John Glynn

117

Je - sus the hea - ler is here in our midst, as he has promised to be, stand- ing a - mong us with arms o -pen wide, giv - ing his love so free .

Chorus

Who could re - fuse such ten - der love ? Where is the per-son so whole? Come all you sick, come all you trou - bled, let Je - sus en-ter your soul.

2. We are all fraught by the cares of the world,
tension and turmoil and din;
now let us rest in his glorious love,
quietly listen to him.

3. We can rely on the power of his love,
brought by his Spirit divine,
cleansing our sins and thus making us whole.
Jesus, all glory is thine.

4. Glorious Father of such perfect love,
given by Jesus your Son,
brought by your Spirit and healing us now,
praise be to God three in One.

Words and Music: Gillian Simpson

118

Jo—seph was an hon- est man, he was an hon- est man. He

pleased the Lord in all his ways be-cause he was an

hon- est man. And God said: "I am choos-ing you, because you

are an hon- est man, to care for the one who'll

bear my son, be- cause you are an hon- est man ".

2. Joseph was a faithful man,
   he was a faithful man.
   He kept the trust the Lord had given
   because he was a faithful man.
   He cared for Mary and her son,
   because he was a faithful man,
   through days of pain and days of fun,
   because he was a faithful man.

3. Joseph was a working man,
   he was a working man.
   He laboured as a carpenter
   because he was a working man.
   And daily at his work he'd be,
   because he was a working man,
   no idler or a shirker he,
   because he was a working man.

4. Joseph was a praying man,
   he was a praying man.
   He walked with God each single day
   because he was a praying man.
   In joy or pain he'd turn to him,
   because he was a praying man,
   if fear did rage or hope grew dim,
   because he was a praying man.

5. Joseph was an honest man,
   he was an honest man.
   His blameless life won it's reward
   because he was an honest man
   The Lord was pleased and called him home
   because he was an honest man,
   with him to rest, no more to roam
   because he was an honest man.

6. Joseph is a helping man,
   he is a helping man.
   He rescues those who turn to him
   because he is a helping man.
   So go to Joseph in your need,
   because he is a helping man,
   you'll see him work with power and speed,
   because he is a helping man.

Words and Music: Sister M. Pereira

119

Peace is the gift of hea-ven to earth, soft-ly en-fol-ding our fears. Peace is the gift of Christ to the world, giv-en for us. He is the Lamb who bore the pain of peace.

2.
Peace is the gift of Christ to his Church,
wound of the lance of his love.
Love is the pain he suffered for man,
offered to us:
Oh, to accept the wound that brings us peace!

3.
Joy is the gift the Spirit imparts,
born of the heavens and earth.
We are his children, children of joy,
people of God:
He is our Lord, our peace, our love, our joy!

Words and Music: John Glynn

120

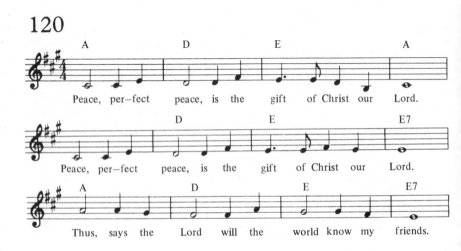

Peace, per-fect peace, is the gift of Christ our Lord.
Peace, per-fect peace, is the gift of Christ our Lord.
Thus, says the Lord will the world know my friends.

Peace, per—fect peace, is the gift of Christ our Lord.

2. Love, perfect love. . .   4. Hope, perfect hope. . .
3. Faith, perfect faith. . .   5. Joy, perfect joy. . .   *Words and Music: Kevin Mayhew*

121

Chorus Am

Peace — ma—kers to be called the sons of God. Peace— ma—kers to be called the sons of God. 1. See — ing the crowd, Je—sus went up to the hill. There he sat down and was joined by his friends. Then he be—gan to speak to them, and this is what he said: You must be

2. Happy the gentle,
   for I give to them the earth.
   Happy the mourners,
   I will comfort their distress.
   Happy are those who thirst and hunger
   after what is right.
   They shall be. . .

Words and Music: Malcolm Campbell-Carr

122 MASS OF PEACE

Lord, have mer-cy on your ser - v°nts. Lord, have mer-cy on your ser - vants.

Lord, have mer-cy on your ser - vants. Lord, have mer-cy on us all.

2. Christ, have mercy on your servants . . .
3. Lord, have mercy on your servants . . .

Sanctus

1. Holy, holy, holy, holy
   God of might and God of power.
   Glory fills all earth and heaven.
   Sing hosanna to the Lord.
2. Blessed is the one who comes,
   comes in glory from the Lord.
   Raise your voices, sing his praises.
   Sing hosanna to the Lord.

Agnus Dei

1. Lamb of God, O Jesus Christ,
   take the sin of all the world.
   Give us mercy, Lamb of God.
   Give us mercy, Lamb of God.
2. Lamb of God, O Jesus Christ,
   take the sin of all the world.
   Grant us peace, O Lamb of God.
   Grant us peace, O Lamb of God.

Words and Music: Adapted from traditional sources by Kevin Mayhew

123 MASS OF THANKSGIVING

Lord, have mer- cy on your ser- vants. Lord, have mer-cy on us all.

God al - migh - ty, just and faith-ful, Lord, have mer-cy on us all.

2. Christ, have mercy on your servants.
   Christ, have mercy on us all.
   Light of truth and light of justice,
   Christ, have mercy on us all.

3. *Repeat Verse 1*

Sanctus

1. Holy, holy, holy, holy
   God of pow'r and God of might.
   Heav'n and earth are filled with glory.
   Sing hosanna to the Lord.

2. Blessed is the one from heaven,
   sent to us from God above.
   Sing hosanna, sing hosanna,
   sing hosanna to the Lord.

Agnus Dei

1. Jesus, Lamb of God, have mercy,
   Jesus, bearer of our sins.
   Take our sins, Lord. Take our sins, Lord.
   Give us mercy, Lamb of God.

2. Jesus, Lamb of God, have mercy,
   Jesus, bearer of our sins.
   Take our sins, Lord. Take our sins, Lord.   *Words and Music: Adapted from traditional*
   Grant us peace, O Lamb of God.   *sources by Kevin Mayhew*

MASS OF THE SPIRIT 124

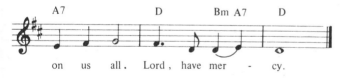

Sanctus

Holy, holy, holy Lord
God of pow'r and might.
Glory fills all heav'n and earth.
Sing hosanna, sing.
Holy, holy, holy, holy.
Blessed is the one who comes.
Sing hosanna, sing.

Agnus Dei

Lamb of God, you take our sin,
show us mercy, Lord.
Lamb of God, you take our sin,
show us mercy, Lord.
Show us mercy, show us mercy.
Lamb of God, you take our sin,
grant us all your peace.

Words and Music: Adapted from traditional sources by Kevin Mayhew

125

Al - le - lu - ia, al - le - lu - ia, al - le - lu - ia, al - le - lu - ia, al - le -
lu - ia, al - le - lu - ia, al - le - lu - ia, al - le - lu - ia.

2. Jesus is Lord. . .

3. And I love him. . .   *Words and Music: Traditional*

126

Al - le - lu - ia, al - le - lu - ia,
al - le - lu - ia, al - le - lu - ia, al - le - lu - ia.

We will   hear your Word, one in   love;   we will   live your Word, one in

love;   we will   spread your Word, one in   love.

Words and Music: Joe Wise

127

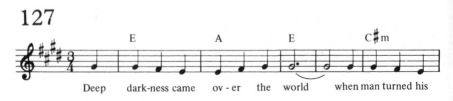

Deep   dark-ness came   ov - er   the   world   when man turned his

back on the Sun. He need-ed no lon-ger the light, could live just as well on his own. But death comes to all in the dark, and man with-out Light is a - lone.

Chorus

But the Sun will shine and true peace will come in the king - dom of our God.

2. Then hate reigned supreme in man's heart,
   the lamb and the kid lived in fear,
   the child could not play with the beast,
   the rivers of love were not clear,
   the chariot of war brought no peace,
   man's life was a tomb of despair.

   But the Sun will shine . . .

3. The Sun did not leave man to die,
   but sent forth the light of new birth.
   A star brought the news of the dawn,
   while darkness still covered the earth.
   Then Light shone again in the world,
   its rays brought dead man back to life

   And the Sun will shine . . .

4. The Sun rose again for all men,
   to shed light on those who were dead,
   to bring love where hatred was strong,
   and peace to where war ruled instead,
   to bring pardon where there was wrong,
   and manna to those without bread.

   And the Sun will shine . . .

5. He came to bring peace to the world,
   to open the eyes of the blind,
   the ears of the deaf were unsealed,
   the tongues of the dumb came to life,
   he came to bring love to the world,
   bring peace till the moon is no more.

   And the Sun will shine . . .

6. Now I am the Light of the world,
   he said to his friends with him then,
   a Sun that must set in the dark,
   a Sun that will rise once again.
   Now you, my dear friends, must go forth,
   to shine with my light among men.

   And the Sun will shine . . .

Words and Music: Michael Evans

128

D   A7   D   G D

1. Let us break bread to- ge-ther on our knees. Let us break bread to-

A E7   A   A7   D   Bm

ge-ther on our knees. When I fall on my knees with my

Em   A7   D Bm Em A7   D G D

face to the ris- ing sun, Oh Lord, have mer- cy on me.

2. Let us drink wine together on our knees. . .

3. Let us praise God together on our knees. . .   *Words and Music: Traditional*

129

G   C   D7 G   C   D7

Like a sea with - out a shore love di- vine is bound-less.

G   C   D7 G   C   D7

Time is now and ev - er- more and his love sur - rounds us.

Chorus G   Em   Am   D7

Ma - ra - na - tha ! Ma - ra - na - tha !

G   **Em**   **C**   **D7**   **G**

Ma - ra - na - tha! Come, Lord Je - sus, come!

2. So that mankind could be free
   he appeared among us.
   Blest are those who have not seen,
   yet believe his promise.

3. All our visions, all our dreams,
   are but ghostly shadows
   of the radiant clarity
   waiting at life's close.

4. Death where is your victory?
   Death where is your sting?
   Closer than the air we breathe
   is our risen King.

'Maranatha' is an Aramaic phrase meaning 'Lord come'
see 1 Corinthians 16:22

Words and Music: Estelle White

130

C   **G7**   **F**   **C**

Like the stars in the sky, like the waves of the sea, you are

G7   **F**   **C**   *Chorus*   **Em**

time - less and age - less and free. Take me now, Lord my

Am   **Dm**   **G7**   **C**

God, take my heart, take my mind, take me bo - dy and

G7   **F**   **C**

soul; make me free.

2. You are good, you are truth,
   you are God for all time,
   you are Lord of all men, you are mine.

3. Send your Spirit of love,
   like a wind blowing free,
   let him fill every corner of me.

4. Lord, I come now with praise,
   Lord, I come to you free,
   for you've given your Spirit to me.

Words and Music: Gillian Simpson

131

They say I am wise and they say I am King. I'm a car-penter's son and I don't own a thing. They say I am rich and they say I am poor, and when I came knocking they bol-ted the door.

2. They asked me for bread and they asked for a sign.
   I gave them some bread and I gave them some wine.
   The bread was my body, the wine was my blood.
   They still turned away from me looking for food.

3. They shouted with joy. They laid palms on the road,
   but into the town on a donkey I rode.
   They said: "Do not go for we can't stand the loss ".
   The very next morning they gave me a cross.

4. They brought me down low though they hung me up high.
   They brought me to life though they left me to die.
   They buried me deep with a stone at my head,
   but I am the living and they are the dead.

Words: Michael Cockett
Music: Kevin Mayhew

132

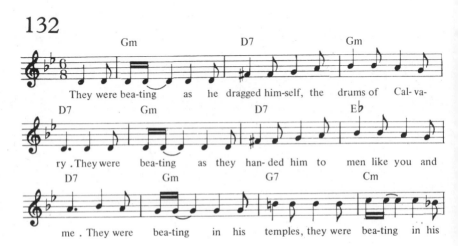

They were bea-ting as he dragged him-self, the drums of Cal-va-ry. They were bea-ting as they han-ded him to men like you and me. They were bea-ting in his temples, they were bea-ting in his

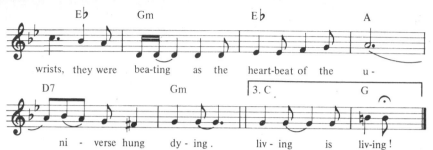

wrists, they were bea-ting as the heart-beat of the u-
ni - verse hung dy - ing . liv - ing is liv-ing!

2. They were beating as they drove the nails,
   the drums of Calvary.
   They were beating as they raised him up
   for everyone to see.
   They were beating in his temples,
   they were beating in his wrists,
   they were beating as the heart-beat of the universe
   hung dying.

3. They are beating now across the world,
   the drums of Calvary.
   They are throbbing and they're pounding out,
   they're calling men to be.
   They beat out in each man's temples,
   they beat out in each man's wrists,
   they are beating as the heart-beat of the universe
   is living, is living, is living!

Words and Music: Estelle White

133

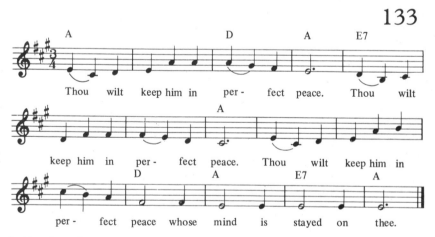

Thou wilt keep him in per - fect peace. Thou wilt
keep him in per - fect peace. Thou wilt keep him in
per - fect peace whose mind is stayed on thee.

2. Marvel not, I say unto you; (3)
   you must be born again.

3. Though your sins as scarlet be, (3)
   they shall be white as snow.

4. If the Son shall set you free, (3)
   you shall be free indeed.

Words and Music: Anonymous

134

Chorus

Yah-weh, you are my strength and sal-va-tion.

Yah-weh, you are my rock and my shield.   1. When

foes in-side my soul as-sailed me,   he

heard my cry for help and came to my aid.

2. He bent the heav'ns and came in thunder.
   He flew to me and soared on wings of the wind.

3. The depths within my mind he showed me,
   the hidden thoughts that I did not know were there.

4. His arm stretched from on high and held me.
   He drew me from the deep, wild waters of self.

5. He is the lamp who lights the darkness.
   He guides me as I leap the ramparts of life.

6. I raise my voice and sing his glory.
   With all my heart I praise the God of my joy.   *Words and Music: Estelle White*

135

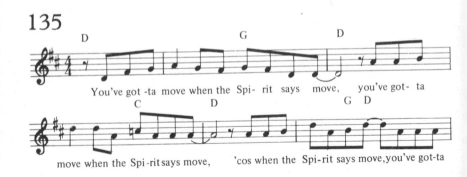

You've got -ta move when the Spi-rit says move,   you've got- ta

move when the Spi-rit says move,   'cos when the Spi-rit says move, you've got-ta

move when the Spi-rit, move when the Spi- rit says move.

2. You've gotta sing . . . 4. You've gotta shout . . . *Words and Music:*

3. You've gotta clap . . . 5. You've gotta jump . . . *Traditional (arr. Kevin Donovan)*

AMERICAN EUCHARIST **136**

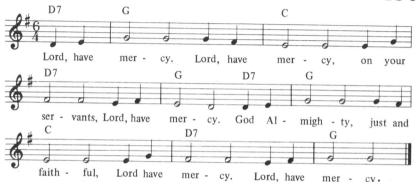

Lord, have mer - cy. Lord, have mer - cy, on your
ser - vants, Lord, have mer - cy. God Al - migh - ty, just and
faith - ful, Lord have mer - cy. Lord, have mer - cy.

Christ, have mercy, Christ, have mercy,
gift from heaven, Christ have mercy.
Light of truth, and light of justice,
Christ, have mercy. Christ have mercy.

Lord, have mercy, Lord, have mercy,
on your servants, Lord, have mercy.
God almight, just and faithful,
Lord, have mercy. Lord, have mercy.

Holy Holy Holy

Holy, holy, holy, holy,
Lord of hosts. You fill with glory
all the earth and all the heavens.
Sing hosanna, sing hosanna.

Blest and holy, blest and holy
he who comes now in the Lord's name.
In the highest sing hosanna,
in the highest sing hosanna.

Lamb of God

Jesus, Lamb of God, have mercy,
bearer of our sins, have mercy. (Repeat)
Saviour of the world, Lord Jesus,
may your peace be with us always. (Repeat)

*Words and Music: Sandra Joan Billington
(adapted from an American folk melody).*

137

There is a world where peo-ple come and go about their ways and
ne-ver care to know that ev-'ry step they take is placed on roads
made out of men who had to car-ry loads too hard to bear.

Chorus

"That world 'c not ours!" That's what we al-ways say: "We'll build a new one
but some oth-er day." When will we wake from com-fort and from ease,
and strive to-geth-er to cre-ate a world of love and peace?

*To give added effect to this song verse two may be played in D, modulating by one bar of
A7, and verse three in E, modulating by one bar of B7.*

2. There is a world where people walk alone,
and have around them men with hearts of stone,
who would not spare one second of their day,
or spend their breath in order just to say: "Your pain is mine."

3. There is a world where brothers cannot meet
with one another where the tramp of feet
brings men of ice, men who would force apart
friends of all races having but one heart, a heart of love.   *Words and Music: Estelle White*

138

There will be signs in the moon and the stars and the sun, the

o - cean seething high and cla-mou-ring, that day the sun will darken, and the

moon will turn to blood, to pro - phe - sy the jud-ging of the world.

Chorus   *No man can tell, nor an angel, the day of the end*
            until the Father says the secret word.
            Be watchful for his coming, Christ the dawn that knows no dark,
            Keep watch and guard with ever-open eyes.

  2. Mankind will come, one and all, when the trumpet shall sound,
     and Christ will set the nations gathering,
     all running to the judgment seat, the living and the dead,
     all summoned by the trumpeter of God.

  3. The Son of Man in his glory will come on the clouds,
     so call upon his name and save yourself;
     lift up your heads in hope to see the Christ who died for you;
     have faith and stand up tall to meet the Lord.

  4. Keep your heart wise, unsullied, your mind free and strong
     in prayer and praise until the Saviour comes,
     as brilliant as the lightening blazing bright across the sky,
     the Lord, the Master, on the day of doom. *Words: Luke Connaughton*
                                Music: Malcolm Campbell-Carr

139

They hung him on a cross, they hung him on a cross, they

hung him on a cross for me. One day when I was lost, they

hung him on a cross, they hung him on a cross for me.

2. They whipped him up the hill. . .   5. He hung his head and died. . .
3. They speared him in the side. . .   6. He's coming back again. . .
4. The blood came streaming down. . .   *Words and Music: Spiritual*

140

Chorus

Where are you bound, Ma - ry, Ma - ry?

Where are you bound, Mo - ther of God? 1. Beau -ty is a

dove sit - ting on a sun - lit bough, beau - ty is a

pray'r with - out the need of words. Words are more than sounds

fal - ling off an emp - ty tongue: Let it be ac -

cor - ding to his word.

2. Mary heard the word spoken in her inmost heart;
   Mary bore the Word and held him in her arms.
   Sorrow she has known, seeing him upon the cross
   — greater joy to see him rise again.

3. Where are we all bound, carrying the Word of God?
   Time and place are ours to make his glory known.
   Mary bore him first, we will tell the whole wide world:
   Let it be according to his word.

Words and Music: John Glynn

Lord, have mer - cy on us all. Lord, have mer - cy

on us. Lord, have mer - cy on us all

Lord, have mer - cy on us.

Christ, have mercy on us all.
Christ, have mercy on us. (Repeat)

Lord, have mercy on us all.
Lord, have mercy on us. (Repeat)

Holy Holy Holy

Holy, holy, holy Lord,
earth is full of your glory.
Glory fills the heavens too.
Sing to him Hosanna!

Blessed is the one who comes
bringing this great glory.
Holy, holy, holy Lord.
Sing to him Hosanna!

Lamb of God

Lamb of God, O Jesus Christ,
take away our sins,
and have mercy on us all,
and have mercy on us. (Repeat)

Lamb of God, O Jesus Christ,
take away our sins.
Grant us peace, O grant us peace,
grant us peace for ever.

*Words and Music: Anthony Hamson
(adapted from a Swedish Folk melody)*

142

Deep peace of the run-ning wave to you,
deep peace of the flow-ing air to you,
deep peace of the qui-et earth to you,
deep peace of the shin-ing stars to you,
deep peace of the Son of peace to you.

Words: Fiona Macleod Music: Robert Kelly

143

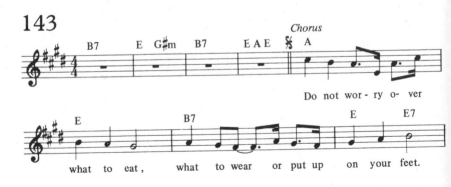

Do not wor-ry o-ver what to eat, what to wear or put up on your feet.

Trust and pray, go do your best to-day, then
leave it in the hands of the Lord.
Leave it in the hands of the Lord.

1. The li-lies of the field, they do not spin or weave, yet
Sol - o - mon was not ar - rayed like one of these. The
birds of the air, they do not sow or reap, but
God tends to them, like a shep- herd tends his sheep.

2. The Lord will guide you in his hidden way,
show you what to do and tell you what to say.
When you pray for rain, go build a dam to store
ev'ry drop of water you have asked him for.

3. The Lord knows all your needs before you ask.
Only trust in him for he will do the task
of bringing in your life whatever you must know.
He'll lead you through the darkness wherever you must go.

Words and Music: Sebastian Temple

144

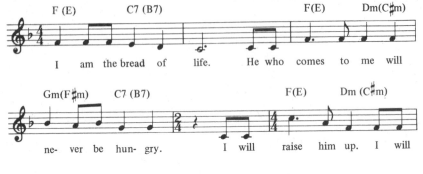

I am the bread of life. He who comes to me will

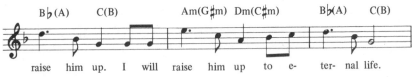

ne- ver be hun- gry. I will raise him up. I will

raise him up. I will raise him up to e- ter- nal life.

I am the bread of life.

2. I am the spring of life.
   He who hopes in me will never be thirsty.
   I will raise him up. . .
   I am the spring of life.

3. I am the way of life.
   He who follows me will never be lonely.
   I will raise him up. . .
   I am the way of life.

4. I am the truth of life.
   He who looks for me will never seek blindly.
   I will raise him up. . .
   I am the truth of life.

5. I am the life of life.
   He who dies with me will never die vainly.
   I will raise him up. . .
   I am the life of life.

Words: David Konstant   Music: Kevin Mayhew

I be-lieve in God a-bove, King and ma-ker of the world. He guides and cares for each of us our Fa-ther and cre-a - tor.

2. I believe in Jesus Christ,
   only Son of God on high.
   The Virgin Mary gave him birth
   by power of the Spirit.

3. I believe in Christ our Lord,
   come to save us from our sins.
   He conquered death and lives again
   to lead us to the Father.

4. I believe in he who comes
   bringing life and truth to all;
   the Holy Spirit, one with God,
   to him we offer glory.

5. I believe in God's one Church,
   source of hope for all mankind.
   As pilgrim saints we'll find life's way,
   and reach our home in heaven.

Words: David Konstant
Music: Music: Kevin Mayhew

The Word in-car-nate sa-cri-ficed his life u-pon the cross and

willed that he should die for one and all, and

through this sa - cri- fice he gave to man what men had lost through that

fate-ful deed which brought a-bout his fall. We of-fer this

bread to you, O Lord, we of-fer this wine, in un-ion with

Christ our Lord and God, we of-fer you praise, we of-fer you

praise.

2. So in this Eucharistic feast we call to mind the love
which God revealed through Christ his only Son.
The Spirit came upon him as a sign from God above
that his mission in the world had just begun.

3. He called the twelve together and he gave them this command:
"You must do this in memory of me.
Each time you eat this food you eat my Body, drink my Blood,
and you offer praise to God the Trinity".

4. O let your Spirit come upon these gifts of bread and wine
   to sanctify this offering in your name,
   and send your Advocate to gather all men into one,
   that in union we may praise your holy name.   *Words and Music: Turloch Holmes*

147

The Vir-gin Ma-ry had a ba-by boy, the
Vir-gin Ma-ry had a ba-by boy, the Vir-gin Ma-ry had a
ba-by boy and they said that his name was Je-sus. He came from the
glo-ry, he came from the glorious kingdom. He came from the
glo-ry, he came from the glo-rious kingdom. Oh yes, be-
lie-ver, Oh yes, be-lie-ver. He came from the
glo-ry, he came from the glo-rious king-dom.

2. The angels sang when the baby was born, (3)
   and proclaimed him the Saviour, Jesus.

3. The wise men saw where the baby was born, (3)
   and they saw that his name was Jesus.   *Words and Music: Traditional West Indian*

148

When Is-rael was in Egypt's land, let my peo-ple go, op-pressed so hard they could not stand, let my peo-ple go. Go down, Mo-ses, way down in Eg-ypt's land. Tell old Phar-oah to let my peo-ple go.

2. The Lord told Moses what to do,
   let my people go,
   to lead the children of Israel through,
   let my people go.

3. Your foes shall not before you stand,
   let my people go,
   and you'll possess fair Canaan's land,
   let my people go.

4. O let us all from bondage flee,
   let my people go,
   and let us all in Christ be free,
   let my people go.

5. I do believe without a doubt,
   let my people go,
   a Christian has a right to shout,
   let my people go.

*Words and Music:
Negro Spiritual*

149

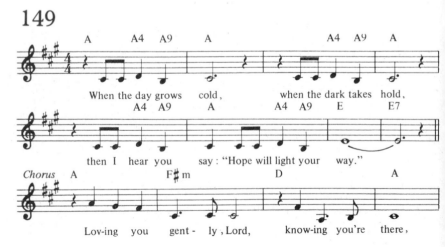

When the day grows cold, when the dark takes hold, then I hear you say: "Hope will light your way." *Chorus* Lov-ing you gent - ly, Lord, know-ing you're there,

find - ing my hope in you, safe in your care.

Lov - ing you gent - ly, Lord, know- ing you're there,

find - ing my hope in you, safe in your care.

2. When the petals fall,
   when the winter calls,
   then I think of you,
   faith will rise anew.
   Loving you gently, Lord,
   knowing you're there,
   finding my faith in you,
   safe in your care. (Repeat)

3. When the gale has blown,
   when the storm has torn,
   then the calm recalls,
   peace that conquers all.
   Loving you gently, Lord,
   knowing you're there,
   finding my peace in you,
   safe in your care. (Repeat)

Words: Michael Cockett
Music: Kevin Mayhew

150

With a song in our hearts we shall go on our way, to bring

God's love to ev' - ry - one we meet to - day. Love, love,

love is his name. Love, love, love is his name. Great, great,

great is his name. Great, great, great is his name. With a

Words and Music: Estelle White

151

Jesus, Lord, I'll sing a song that's soft and low for you, so you can join with me and sing it too. You have said that when we pray, then you are praying too, and when your Father hears us, he hears you.

Chorus

Our Father who art in heaven. hallowed be thy name, hallowed be thy name.

2. I believe that you are here
with me and praying too.
Your Father loves me
because I love you.
Jesus, Lord, I'll sing a song that's
soft and low for you,
so you can join with me
and sing it too.

Words and Music: Briege O'Hare

Long a- go in Beth- le- hem, you were ly- ing

in a man- ger in the midst of hu- man dan- ger,

at your moth- er's knee. Ho- san- na, al- le- lu- ia,

ho- san- na, al- le- lu- ia, ho- san- na,

al- le- lu- ia, at your moth- er's knee.

2. Now as King we hail the baby,
   living faith proclaims the story
   of that humble manger glory,
   stabled in the hay.
   Hosanna, alleluia. . .
   Christ is King today.

Words and Music: Ian Sharp
(arranged from Papuan sources)

153

The Spi-rit of the Lord is now up-on me

to heal the bro-ken heart and set the cap tives free,

to op-en pri-son doors and make the blind to see.

The Spi-rit of the Lord is now on me.

Words and Music: Anonymous

154

There is a ri-ver that flows from God a-

bove; there is a foun-tain that's filled with

his great love. Come to the wa-ters, there

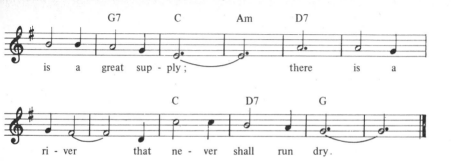

is a great sup - ply ; there is a
ri - ver that ne - ver shall run dry.

Words and Music: Anonymous

155

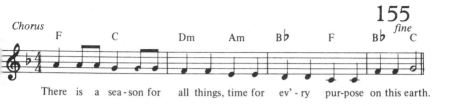

Chorus

There is a sea - son for all things, time for ev' - ry pur - pose on this earth.

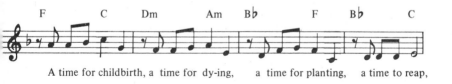

A time for childbirth, a time for dy-ing, a time for planting, a time to reap,

a time for sorrow, a time for laughter, a time for dancing, a time to weep.

2. A time for building, a time to break down,
a time for tearing, a time to bind,
a time for closeness, a time for distance,
a time for losing, a time to find.

3. A time for killing, a time for healing,
a time for speaking, a time to cease,
a time for loving, a time for hating,
a time for fighting, a time for peace.

Words (based on Ecclesiastes): Francesca Leftley   Music: Pachelbell's Canon

156

Lion of Ju - dah, Lamb of peace, Da-vid's son and love's High Priest,

al- le - lu - ia, al - le - lu –ia, al - le - lu - ia, Lord of all, be- come the least.

2. Servant King whose love was shown,
   crowned with thorns and cross as throne,
   alleluia, alleluia, alleluia,
   Lamb-king slain and sealed with stone.

3. King of brightness, fount of light,
   Easter flame to end our night,
   alleluia, alleluia, alleluia,
   holy is the Lord of might.

4. King of glory, King of kings,
   all the earth in union sings,
   alleluia, alleluia, alleluia,
   praise our God whose reign Christ brings.

5. Lion of Judah, Lamb of peace,
   share with us your royal feast,
   alleluia, alleluia, alleluia,
   kingdom come and never cease.

Words and Music: Michael Evans

157

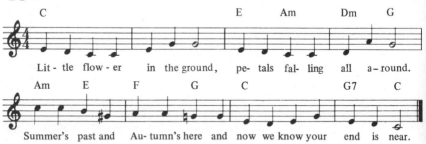

Lit - tle flow - er in the ground, pe - tals fal- ling all a – round.

Summer's past and Au- tumn's here and now we know your end is near.

2. Seeds that fall on to the ground
   by the winds are scattered round.
   Some will feed the Winter birds,
   and some will nestle in the earth.

3. Some will last the Winter through
   'till the Spring makes all things new.
   See the flower newly grown
   from seeds the Winter wind has sown.

4. Praise the Lord in heav'n above,
   who shows us all the way of love.
   Praise him for the dying year.
   If Winter comes then Spring is near.

Words: Michael Cockett
Music: Kevin Mayhew

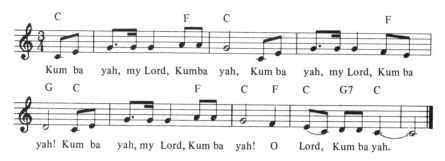

Kum ba yah, my Lord, Kumba yah, Kum ba yah, my Lord, Kum ba yah! Kum ba yah, my Lord, Kum ba yah! O Lord, Kum ba yah.

2. Someone's crying, Lord, kum ba yah. . .

3. Someone's singing, Lord, kum ba yah. . .

4. Someone's praying, Lord, kum ba yah. . .

Words and Music: Spiritual

Let all that is with- in me cry ho- ly. Let all that is with- in me cry ho- ly. Ho- ly, ho- ly, ho- ly is the Lamb that was slain.

2. Let all that is within me cry mighty. (2)
   Mighty, mighty, mighty is the Lamb that was slain.

3. Let all that is within me cry worthy. (2)
   Worthy, worthy, worthy is the Lamb that was slain.

4. Let all that is within me cry blessed. (2)
   Blessed, blessed, blessed is the Lamb that was slain.

5. Let all that is within me cry Jesus. (2)
   Jesus, Jesus, Jesus is the Lamb that was slain.

Words and Music: Traditional
arr. Kevin Mayhew

160

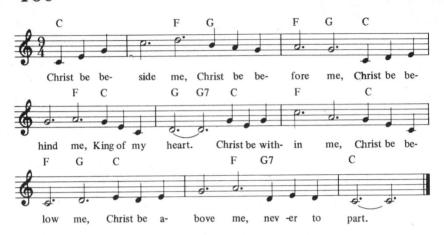

Christ be be- side me, Christ be be- fore me, Christ be be-
hind me, King of my heart. Christ be with- in me, Christ be below me, Christ be a- bove me, nev -er to part.

2. Christ on my right hand,
   Christ on my left hand,
   Christ all around me,
   shield in the strife.
   Christ in my sleeping,
   Christ in my sitting,
   Christ in my rising,
   light of my life.

3. Christ be in all hearts
   thinking about me,
   Christ be in all tongues
   telling of me.
   Christ be the vision
   in eyes that see me,
   in ears that hear me,
   Christ ever be.

Words: Adapted from 'St. Patrick's Breastplate' by James Quinn
Music: Traditional Gaelic melody

161

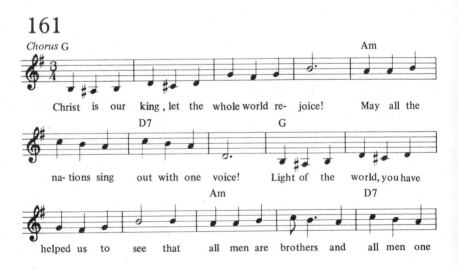

Chorus

Christ is our king, let the whole world re- joice! May all the
na- tions sing out with one voice! Light of the world, you have
helped us to see that all men are brothers and all men one

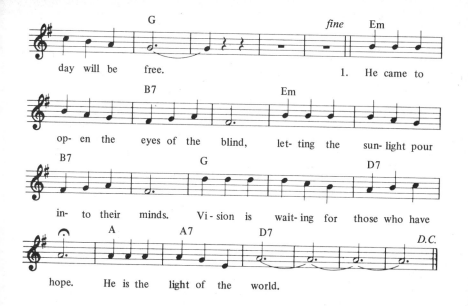

day will be free.   1. He came to op- en the eyes of the blind, let- ting the sun- light pour in- to their minds. Vi - sion is wait- ing for those who have hope. He is the light of the world.

2. He came to speak tender words to the poor,
   he is the gateway and he is the door.
   Riches are waiting for all those who hope.
   He is the light of the world.

3. He came to open the doors of the gaol,
   he came to help the downtrodden and frail.
   Freedom is waiting for all those who hope.
   He is the light of the world.

4. He came to open the lips of the mute,
   letting them speak out with courage and truth.
   His words are uttered by all those who hope.
   He is the light of the world.

5. He came to heal all the crippled and lame,
   sickness took flight at the sound of his name.
   Vigour is waiting for all those who hope.
   He is the light of the world.

6. He came to love every man on this earth
   and through his Spirit he promised rebirth.
   New life is waiting for all those who hope.
   He is the light of the world.

Words and Music: Estelle White

162

We be-lieve in God, the al-migh-ty one, the Fa-ther and Cre-a-tor, Lord of earth and hea-ven. We be-lieve in Je-sus, his on-ly Son. Our Lord born of Ma-ry the mai-den.

2. Jesus is the Lord who was crucified.
   He died upon a cross to bring us to salvation.
   When they came with oils to anoint the Lord
   they found that their loved-one had risen.

3. He it is who sits at the Father's hand,
   the Lord and the annointed conqueror of darkness.
   He will come in glory to judge us all.
   His kingdom will last now and always.

4. We believe he dwells in the Spirit now,
   the Holy One, the Spirit-Love that conquers evil.
   Through the church he left he will make us one,
   forgiving our sins in his mercy.

5. We believe in life that will never end,
   the life that we will live with all the saints of heaven.
   Jesus, Lord and King, who was crucified
   has brought us to life everlasting.

Words: Michael Cockett   Music: John Googe

163

We shall o-ver-come,   We shall o-ver-come,   We shall o-ver-

come some day. Oh, deep in my heart I do be-

lieve that we shall o-ver-come some day.

2. We'll walk hand in hand, (2)
   we'll walk hand in hand some day.
   Oh, deep in my heart I do believe
   that we'll walk hand in hand some day.

3. We shall live in peace. . .

4. We shall live with him. . .

Words and Music: Traditional

164

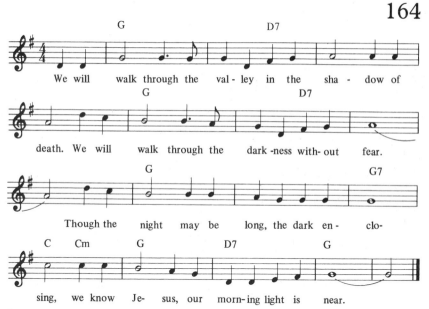

We will walk through the val - ley in the sha - dow of

death. We will walk through the dark -ness with- out fear.

Though the night may be long, the dark en - clo-

sing, we know Je- sus, our morn-ing light is near.

2. He has walked through the valley of the shadow of death,
   he has walked through the night of fear alone.
   Though the darkness had gathered to destroy him
   he was there at the rising of the sun.

3. We will walk in the glory of the bright morning sun,
   we will walk in the light that guides our way.
   For with Jesus the lord of light beside us
   we will walk in the glory of the day.

Words: Michael Cockett
Music: Spiritual adapted by Kevin Mayhew

165 MONMOUTHSHIRE MASS

Lord, have mer-cy on us all. Lord, have mer-cy on us.

Lord, have mer-cy on us all. Lord, have mer-cy on us.

Christ, have mercy on us all.
Christ have mercy on us. (Repeat)

Lord, have mercy on us all.
Lord, have mercy on us. (Repeat)

Holy Holy Holy   *Lamb of God*

Holy, holy, holy Lord,   Lamb of God, you take away
God of might and power.   the sins of all the world.
Glory fills all heav'n and earth.   Lamb of God, you take away
Sing to him Hosanna!   the sins of all the world.

Blessed is the one who comes   Lamb of God, you take away
bringing this great glory.   the sins of all the world.
Praise and honour be to God.   Grant us peace, O Lamb of God,
Sing to him Hosanna!   grant us peace for ever.

Words and Music: Anthony Hamson
(adapted from a Welsh folk melody)

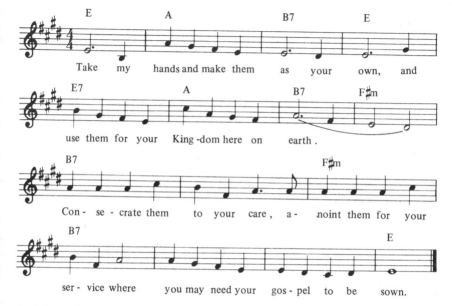

Take my hands and make them as your own, and use them for your King-dom here on earth. Con-se-crate them to your care, a-noint them for your ser-vice where you may need your gos-pel to be sown.

2. Take my hands. They speak now for my heart,
   and by their actions they will show their love.
   Guard them on their daily course,
   be their strength and guiding force
   to ever serve the Trinity above.

3. Take my hands. I give them to you, Lord.
   Prepare them for the service of your name.
   Open them to human need
   and by their love they'll sow your seed
   so all may know the love and hope you give.

Optional ending

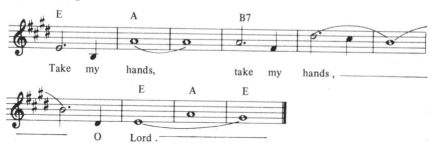

Take my hands, take my hands, O Lord.

Words and Music: Sebastian Temple

167

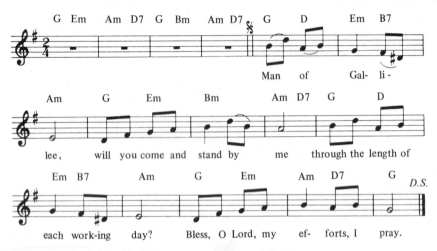

Man of Galli-lee, will you come and stand by me through the length of each working day? Bless, O Lord, my efforts, I pray.

2. Man who healed the blind
   open up the eyes of my mind
   to the needs of my fellow man.
   Help me give with open hands.

3. Man of bread and of wine
   show me by the means of this sign
   that I share your life and your light
   with the neighbour here at my side.

Man of Calvary
give me strength and will to be free
of the weight of self-pity's chains,
then my trials will be but gains.

5. Man at God's right hand,
   will you help me understand
   that in you, when my breath is stilled,
   all my longings will be fulfilled?

Words and Music: Estelle White

168

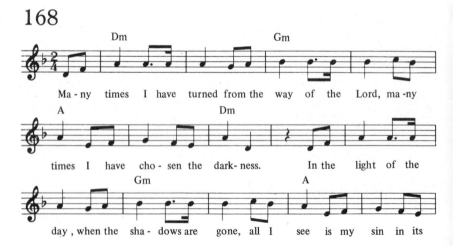

Many times I have turned from the way of the Lord, many times I have chosen the darkness. In the light of the day, when the shadows are gone, all I see is my sin in its

stark - ness. Je - sus came to bring us mer -
cy. Je - sus came to bring us life a - gain. He
loves us, he loves us, he loves us!

2. I confess I have sinned in the sight of the Lord,
   through my pride, through my malice and weakness.
   I've rejected the promise that comes from the cross
   where the Lord hung above us in meakness.

3. With a word, with a deed, with a failure to act,
   with a thought that was evil and hateful,
   I confess to you, brothers and sisters of mine,
   I have sinned and been proven ungrateful.

4. Through my fault, through my fault, through my serious fault,
   I confess to you, Lord, all my sinning.
   But look down on me, Lord, grant your pardon and peace;
   with your help, I've a new life beginning.

Words: Willard F. Jabusch
Music: Russian Folk Melody

169

May the peace of Christ be with you to - day, may the
peace of Christ be with you to - day, may the
love of Christ, the joy of Christ, may the peace of Christ be yours.

Words and Music: Kevin Mayhew

170

Capo 3

Trust is in the eyes of a ti-ny babe
lean-ing on his mother's breast. In the ea-ger beat of a
young bird's wings on the day it leaves the nest. It is the
liv-ing Spi-rit fil-ling the earth, bringing to birth a world of
love and laugh-ter, joy in the light of the Lord.

2. Hope is in the rain that makes crystal streams
   tumble down a mountain side,
   and in every man who repairs his nets,
   waiting for the rising tide.
3. Love is in the hearts of all those who seek
   freedom for the human race.
   Love is in the touch of the hand that heals,
   and the smile that lights a face.
4. Strength is in the wind as it bends the trees,
   warmth is in the bright red flame,
   light is in the sun and the candle-glow,
   cleansing are the ocean's waves.

Words and Music: Estelle White

171

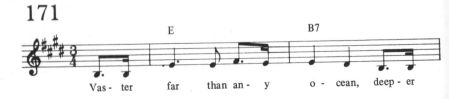

Vas-ter far than an-y o-cean, deep-er

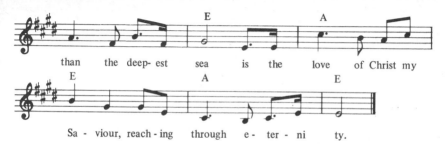

than the deep-est sea is the love of Christ my Sa-viour, reach-ing through e-ter-ni-ty.

2. But my sins are truly many,
   is God's grace so vast, so deep?
   Yes, there's grace o'er sin abounding,
   grace to pardon, grace to keep.

3. Can he quench my thirst for ever?
   Will his Spirit strength impart?
   Yes, he gives me living water
   springing up within my heart.

Words: Author unknown   Music: Russian Folk Tune

172

We are gath-er-ing to-ge-ther un-to him.

We are ga-thering to-ge-ther un-to him.

Un-to him shall the gath'ring of the peo-ple be. We are gath-er-ing to-ge-ther un-to him.

2. We are offering together unto him. . .

Other verses may be added at will:

We are singing together. . .

We are praying together. . .   *Words and Music: Anonymous*

173

Leader
Glo-ry to God, glo-ry to God, glo-ry to the Fa-ther.

All
Glo-ry to God, glo-ry to God, glo-ry to the Fa-ther.

Leader ... *All*
To him be glo-ry for ev-er. To him be

Leader ... *All*
glo-ry for ev-er. Al-le-lu-ia, a-men. Al-le-lu-ia, a-men,

al-le-lu-ia, a-men, al-le-lu-ia, a-men.

2. Glory to God, glory to God,
Son of the Father.
To him. . .

3. Glory to God, glory to God,
glory to the Spirit.
To him. . .

Music: Peruvian

*This song is best sung accompanied only by bongos or a similar percussion instrument.
The optional harmony notes give added effect, but those singing the tune should
remain on the lower notes.*

174

C   F   G   C   F   Dm   G
Glo-ry we sing to God on high, peace on earth to all his friends. We

C   F   G   C   F   G   C7
thank, we praise, we wor-ship him, Lord God, our King and Fa-ther.

Glo - ry, glo - ry, glo - ry we sing to God on high.

2. His only Son, Lord Jesus Christ,
   Lord of all, the Lamb of God,
   who saves the world from all its sin,
   to him we pray for mercy.

3. Glory to you, the Holy One!
   Glory to you, the only Lord!
   To God be glory, Christ most high,
   The Spirit and the Father.

Words: David Konstant Music: Kevin Mayhew

175

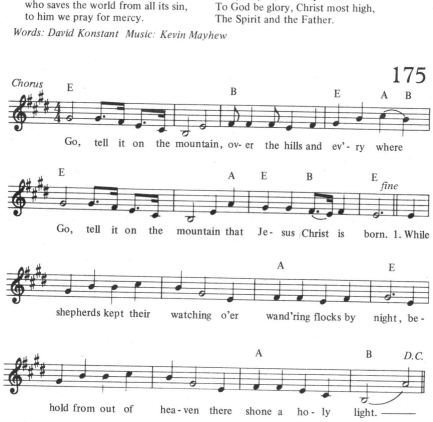

Go, tell it on the mountain, ov- er the hills and ev' - ry where

Go, tell it on the mountain that Je - sus Christ is born. 1. While

shepherds kept their watching o'er wand'ring flocks by night, be -

hold from out of hea - ven there shone a ho - ly light. ———

2. And lo, when they had seen it, they all bowed down and prayed;
   they travelled on together to where the Babe was laid. . .

3. When I was a seeker, I sought both night and day:
   I asked my Lord to help me and he showed me the way. . .

4. He made me a watchman upon the city wall,
   And if I am a Christian, I am the least of all. . .

Words and Music: Traditional

176

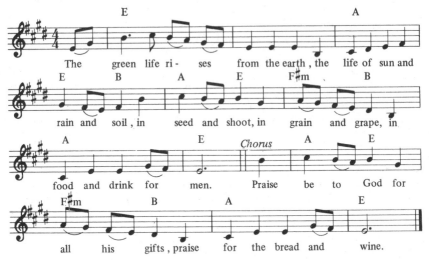

The green life ri - ses from the earth, the life of sun and rain and soil, in seed and shoot, in grain and grape, in food and drink for men. Praise be to God for all his gifts, praise for the bread and wine.

2. The Lord of Spring, the Lord of Life,
made bread his body, wine his blood.
The life of earth, the life of God,
becomes the life of man.

3. We take in hand the bread and wine,
reminder of the dying Lord.
This food, this drink, this feast of joy
gives Christ's own life to us.

4. "The Son of Man must die," said he,
"my death will raise you all to life.
No blade is born, no harvest reaped,
until the seed has died.

5. "These are the signs of death and life,
the bread you break, the cup you share:
my dying gift in which I live,
my death is life to you."

6. Give praise to God who gave this gift,
his very Son, to bring us life.
The Father's life in him is ours,
his Spirit breathes in us.

Words: Luke Connaughton
Music: Traditional English Folk Melody

177

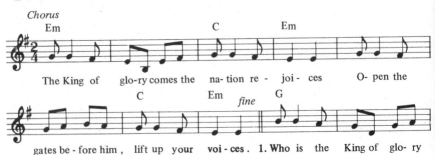

Chorus

The King of glo-ry comes the na-tion re - joi - ces O- pen the gates be - fore him, lift up your voi - ces. 1. Who is the King of glo - ry

how shall we call him? He is Em - ma- nu- el, the promised of a- ges.

2. In all of Galilee,
   in city and village,
   he goes among his people,
   curing their illness.

4. He gave his life for us,
   the pledge of salvation.
   He took upon himself
   the sins of the nation.

3. Sing then of David's Son,
   our Saviour and brother;
   in all of Galilee
   was never another.

5. He conquered sin and death;
   he truly has risen.
   And he will share with us
   his heavenly vision.

Words: W.F. Jabusch
Music: Israeli Folk Song

178

The far - mer in the fer - tile field is sow - ing, sow - ing. The seed is good, the shoots of corn are grow - ing, grow - ing, grow - ing, grow- ing.

2. An enemy with darnel seed is
   sowing, sowing.
   The weed that fights the growing corn is
   choking, choking, choking, choking.

3. Together till the harvest they'll be
   growing, growing.
   But then what has been sown we will be
   reaping, reaping, reaping, reaping.

4. The corn is taken to the barn for
   storing, storing.
   The weed is cast into the fire for
   burning, burning, burning, burning.

Words: Michael Cockett
Music: Roger Haines and John Murphy

179

Mer - ri - ly on, mer - ri - ly on flow the bright

wa - ters that car - ry a song, a song that is sung of the

love of the Lord, a love that is end - less and ev - er out-

poured.

2. Father above, Father above,
   source of our life and our strength and our love,
   as fresh as the spring that is limpid and clear,
   your presence is young and will always be near.

3. Son from on high, Son from on high,
   you who united the earth and the sky,
   Oh, cleanse us with water and fill us with peace,
   our river of mercy who never will cease.

4. Spirit of God, Spirit of God,
   breathe on the waters and flow in the flood,
   and open the flood-gates that lead to the sea
   — the ocean is open and boundless and free!

5. Repeat verse 1.

   Words and Music: John Glynn

Chorus

What-so- ev-er you do to the least of my bro - thers,

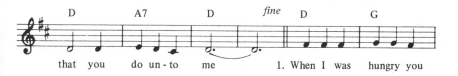

that you do un - to me 1. When I was hungry you

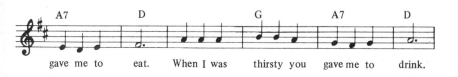

gave me to eat. When I was thirsty you gave me to drink.

Now en - ter in - to the home of my Fa - ther.

2. When I was homeless
   you opened your door.
   When I was naked
   you gave me your coat.
   Now enter into. . . .

3. When I was weary
   you helped me find rest.
   When I was anxious
   you calmed all my fears.
   Now enter into. . . .

4. When in a prison
   you came to my cell.
   When on a sick bed
   you cared for my needs.

5. Hurt in a battle
   you bound up my wounds.
   Searching for kindness
   you held out your hands.

6. When I was Negro
   or Chinese or White,
   mocked and insulted.
   you carried my cross.

7. When I was aged
   you bothered to smile.
   When I was restless
   you listened and cared.

8. When I was laughed at
   you stood by my side.
   When I was happy
   you shared in my Joy.

Words and Music: W.F. Jabusch

181

D · D7 · G · A7

Lord, Je-sus Christ, you have come to us you are

D · Bm · E · A · Em · A7

one with us, Ma-ry's Son. Clean–sing our souls from

D · Bm · Em · A7 · Bm · B7

all their sin, pour–ing your love and good-ness in,

Em · Gm · D · B7 · Em · A7 · D

Je-sus our love for you we sing, liv-ing Lord.

2. Lord Jesus Christ,
   now and ev'ry day
   teach us how to pray, Son of God.
   You have commanded us to do
   this in remembrance, Lord, of you
   Into our lives your pow'r breaks through,
   living Lord.

3. Lord Jesus Christ,
   You have come to us,
   born as one of us, Mary's Son.
   Led out to die on Calvary,
   risen from death to set us free,
   living Lord Jesus, help us see
   you are Lord.

4. Lord Jesus Christ,
   I would come to you,
   live my life for you, Son of God.
   All your commands I know are true,
   your many gifts will make me new,
   into my life your pow'r breaks through,
   living Lord.

Words and Music: Patrick Appleford

182

Capo 1 D · B7 · Em

Lord of the u-ni-verse, you walked up - on this earth, you

A7 · D

knew, like me, the sor-rows and the joys that li-ving brings.

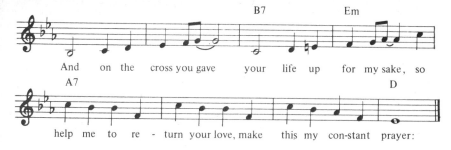

And on the cross you gave your life up for my sake, so help me to re-turn your love, make this my con-stant prayer:

2. Lord, teach me how to serve,
   gladly, as you deserve,
   to give and not to count the cost,
   to fight, not heeding pain.
   may I not seek for rest,
   may I give of my best,
   and ask for no reward save that
   I know I do your will.

Words (based on the prayer of St. Ignatius of Loyola) and Music: Estelle White

183

Lord our God, O Lord our Fa-ther, Lord of love and Lord of fear, now we ga-ther round your al-tar and we know your Word is near.

2. All our lives lie open to you,
   Lord of age and Lord of youth,
   as we bring our sins and falsehoods
   to the judgement of your truth.

3. Lord of times and Lord of seasons,
   Lord of calmness, Lord of stress,
   heart that sees our secret terrors,
   Lord of strength and gentleness.

4. Lord of storms and Lord of sunsets,
   Lord of darkness, Lord of light,
   cast the shadow of your blessing
   on us gathered in your sight.

5. Lord of foes and Lord of friendships,
   Lord of laughter, Lord of tears,
   Lord of toil and Lord of Sabbath,
   Master of the hurrying years.

6. Lord of hope and Lord of hunger,
   Lord of atoms, Lord of space,
   take this world we bring before you
   to the haven of your grace.

Words: Kevin Nichols
Music: Malcolm Campbell-Carr

184

Chorus

Ask, and you will re - ceive. —— Seek, and you will find. —— Knock, and the door will be o - pened for the love of the Lord has no end. 1. Is there an - y man here, when his son asks for bread, would turn him a - way with a stone in - stead? Is there an - y man here, when his son asks for meat, would then give him a poi - son - ous snake to eat?

2. So then how could your Father in heaven above,
   who knows so much more of the ways of love,
   so then how could your Father refuse what is good,
   when you ask in the name of the Son he loves?

3. So whatever you ask you will always receive,
   whatever you seek you will always find.
   For my Father will give to all those who believe
   in the Spirit of love that will never end.

Words: Michael Cockett
Music: Kevin Mayhew

2. Where shall we find bread for the millions almost dead?
   Oh where shall we find bread for the earth?
   Who can dare to speak of the unity we seek?
   Oh where shall we find bread and new birth?

3. Who had loaves and fishes for the hungry and their wishes?
   Oh where shall we find bread or we die?
   Master with thy blessing, break the loaves to us confessing,
   and to the needy world passing by.

Words and Music: Ewald Bash

186

Chorus

Take our bread, we ask you, take our hearts, we love you, take our lives, oh Father, we are yours, we are yours. 1. Yours as we stand at the ta-ble you set, yours as we eat the bread our hearts can't for-get. We are the signs of your life with us yet; we are yours, we are yours.

2. Your holy people stand washed in your blood,
   Spirit filled, yet hungry, we await your food.
   Poor though we are, we have brought ourselves to you:
   we are yours, we are yours.

Words and Music: Joseph Wise

187

The ba - ker wo- man in her hum - ble lodge re-ceived a grain of wheat from God. For nine whole months the

grain she stored . Be - hold the handmaid of the Lord. Make us the bread

Ma - ry , Ma - ry . Make us the bread , we need to be fed .

2. The bakerwoman took the road which led
   to Bethlehem, the house of bread.
   To knead the bread she laboured through the night,
   and brought it forth about midnight.
   Bake us the bread, Mary, Mary.
   Bake us the bread, we need to be fed.

3. She baked the bread for thirty years
   by the fire of her love and the salt of her tears,
   by the warmth of a heart so tender and bright,
   and the bread was golden brown and white.
   Bring us the bread, Mary, Mary.
   Bring us the bread, we need to be fed.

4. After thirty years the bread was done.
   It was taken to the town by her only son;
   the soft white bread to be given free
   to the hungry people of Galilee.
   Give us the bread, Mary, Mary.
   Give us the bread, we need to be fed.

5. For thirty coins the bread was sold,
   and a thousand teeth so cold, so cold
   tore it to pieces on a Friday noon
   when the sun turned black and red the moon.
   Break us the bread, Mary, Mary.
   Break us the bread, we need to be fed.

6. And when she saw the bread so white,
   the living bread she had made at night,
   devoured as wolves might devour a sheep,
   the bakerwoman began to weep.
   Weep for the bread, Mary, Mary.
   Weep for the bread, we need to be fed.

7. But the bakerwoman's only son
   appeared to his friends when three days had run
   on the road which to Emmaus led,
   and they knew him in the breaking of bread.
   Lift up your head, Mary, Mary.
   Lift up your head, for now we've been fed.

Words: Translated from the French by Hubert Richards
Music: Hubert Richards

188

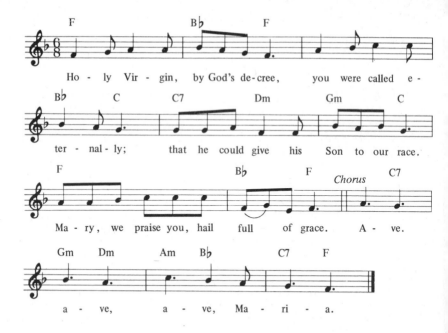

Ho - ly Vir - gin, by God's de-cree, you were called e -
ter - nal - ly; that he could give his Son to our race.
Ma - ry, we praise you, hail full of grace. A - ve.
a - ve, a - ve, Ma - ri - a.

Chorus

2. By your faith and loving accord,
   as the handmaid of the Lord,
   you undertook God's plan to embrace.
   Mary, we thank you, hail full of grace.

3. Refuge for your children so weak,
   sure protection all can seek.
   Problems of life you help us to face.
   Mary, we trust you, hail full of grace.

4. To our needy world of today
   love and beauty you portray,
   showing the path to Christ we must trace.
   Mary, our mother, hail, full of grace.

Words: J. P. Lécot, tr. W. Raymond Lawrence
Music: Abbé P. Decha

189

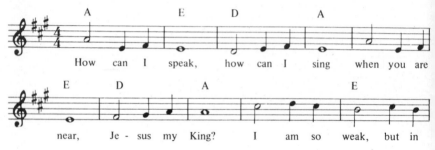

How can I speak, how can I sing when you are
near, Je - sus my King? I am so weak, but in

you I am strong: you be my voice, you be my song.

2. How can I move, how can I see?
   Only if you stay near to me.
   With you I rest, and with you I arise:
   you be my hands, you be my eyes.

3. I give you all, all that is mine,
   yet 'tis no gift, 'tis but a sign:
   I only give what you first gave to me:
   you are my gift, ever to be.

Words and Music: John Glynn

190

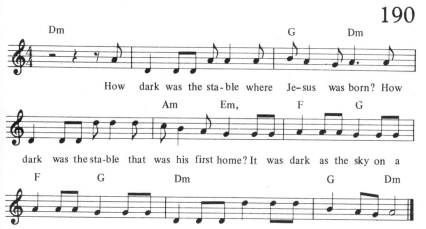

How dark was the sta-ble where Je-sus was born? How

dark was the sta-ble that was his first home? It was dark as the sky on a

black winter's night, when the stars will not shine and the moon gives no light.

2. How cold was the stable where Jesus was born?
   How cold was the stable that was his first home?
   It was cold as the frost on a white window pane;
   It was cold as a heart that has known no love.

3. How light was the stable when Jesus was born?
   How light was the stable he made his first home?
   It was light as the star that was shining that night;
   it was light as an angel in splendour and might.

4. How warm was the stable when Jesus was born?
   How warm was the stable he made his first home?
   It was warm as the love of that first Christmas morn;
   It was warm as our hearts in which Jesus is born.

Words: Michael Cockett
Music: Kevin Mayhew

191

Chorus   D

Walk with me, oh my Lord, through the dark-est

A7   Em   A7

night and brightest day.   Be at my side, oh Lord,

D   *fine*

hold my hand and guide me on my way.

Bm   F#m   Bm   F#m

1. Some-times the road seems long, my en-er-gy is spent.

Bm   F#m   E7   A7   *D.C.*

Then, Lord, I think of you and I am gi-ven strength.

2. Stones often bar my path
and there are times I fall,
but you are always there
to help me when I call.

3. Just as you calmed the wind
and walked upon the sea,
conquer, my living Lord,
the storms that threaten me.

4. Help me to pierce the mists
that cloud my heart and mind
so that I shall not fear
the steepest mountain-side.

5. As once you healed the lame
and gave sight to the blind,
help me when I'm downcast
to hold my head up high.

Words and Music: Estelle White

192

D   Bm   Em   A   D   Bm

Ah —— Ah —— Ah ———— 1. Where would we be without

Em A D Bm Em A

Christ our Lord? We would be lost and walk-ing in dark-ness

Eb F Eb F G Dm

He is the lantern that lights up that darkness and he is the shepherd who

G A D Bm A Em D A Bm A

Chorus

finds the right path. So let the trumpet sound to the glo-ry of God.

Bm G A D Bm Em A

fine

He is our Lord, loving and wise.

2.
Where would we be without Christ our Lord?
We would be left to wander the desert.
He is the beacon that leads us to safety,
and he is the water that brings us new life.

3.
Where would we be without Christ our Lord?
We would be cold and starving and thirsty.
He is the bread that is food for the spirit,
and he is the wine of the new covenant.

4.
Where would we be without Christ our Lord?
He is the Son who saves all the nations.
Through Christ the Son we are given the Spirit,
and this is the Spirit who brings us new life.

Words: Michael Cockett Music: Kevin Mayhew

193

Am D7 G Bm

We bring our gifts to the Lord, our God.

Am D7 G C G

we bring our gifts to the Lord, our God.

2. We bring our love to the Lord, our God. *(Repeat)*

3. We bring ourselves to the Lord, our God. *(Repeat)*

Words and Music: Estelle White

194

Chorus

Sing, sing, sing, sing, sing, sing! Sing! peo- ple of

God, sing! Sing with one ac - cord. Sing! people of

God, sing your prais - es to the Lord. ——— *fine*

1. O Lord, how glo - ri - ous o - ver all the good earth is your

name. You have ex - al·ted your maj - es - ty o- ver ev'- ry hill and

plain. From the mouths of the lit - tle ones you

fash - ion end - less praise to si - lence all the

venge - ful ones and glo - ri - fy your ways.

2. When we behold the heavens
   where your creation shines,
   the moon and stars you set in place
   to stand the test of time,
   what is man that you should mind,
   his sons that you should care?
   A little less than angels
   you have crowned him ev'rywhere.

3. You've given us dominion
   over all that you have made.
   We're masters of your handiwork
   and rule them unafraid.
   We're lords of the fish and birds,
   of beasts both wild and tame.
   O Lord, how glorious over all
   the good earth is your name.

Words and Music: Sebastian Temple

195

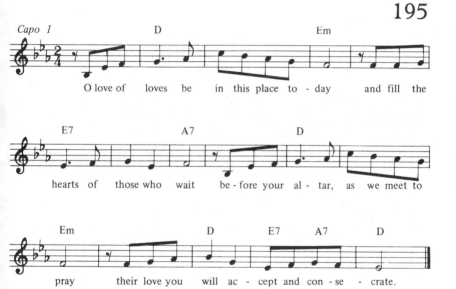

O love of loves be in this place to - day and fill the hearts of those who wait be - fore your al - tar, as we meet to pray their love you will ac - cept and con - se - crate.

2. O hope of hopes may this, your Sacrament,
   be heaven's sign that their request
   is granted wholly, and that you consent
   to share their life and make their union blest.

3. O strength of strengths, with bonds that will not break,
   join these your servants, make them one.
   In joy and sorrow may they have the grace
   to lean upon you, Jesus Christ the Son.

Words and Music: Estelle White

196

Morn-ing has bro-ken like the first morn-ing, blackbird has
spo-ken like the first bird. Praise for the sing-ing! Praise for the
morn-ing! Praise for them, spring-ing fresh from the Word!

2. Sweet the rain's new fall
sunlit from heaven,
like the first dew-fall
on the first grass.
Praise for the sweetness
of the wet garden,
sprung in completeness
where his feet pass.

3. Mine is the sunlight!
Mine is the morning
born of the one light
Eden saw play!
Praise with elation,
praise ev'ry morning,
God's re-creation
of the new day!

Words: Eleanor Farjeon
Music: Traditional Gaelic melody

197

My God loves me. His love will
ne-ver end. He rests within my heart for my God loves me.

2. His gentle hand
   he stretches over me.
   Though storm-clouds threaten the day
   he will set me free.

3. He comes to me
   in sharing bread and wine.
   He brings me life that will reach
   past the end of time.

4. My God loves me,
   his faithful love endures.
   And I will live like a child
   held in love secure.

5. The joys of love
   as offerings now we bring.
   The pains of love will be lost
   in the praise we sing.

Words: Verse 1 Anonymous
Verses 2-5 Sandra Joan Billington
Music: 'Plaisir d'Amour'

198

My glo-ry and the lif-ter of my head, my glo-ry and the lif-ter of my head, for thou, O Lord, art a shield to me, my glo-ry and the lif-ter of my head. I cried un-to the Lord with my voice, I cried un-to the Lord with my voice, I cried un-to the Lord with my voice and he heard me out of his ho-ly hill.

Words: From Scripture
Music: M.J. McAlister

199

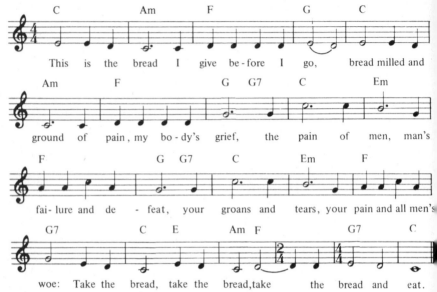

This is the bread I give be-fore I go, bread milled and ground of pain, my bo-dy's grief, the pain of men, man's fai-lure and de-feat, your groans and tears, your pain and all men's woe: Take the bread, take the bread, take the bread and eat.

2. This is the cup that bought the world again,
   red with the wine my hands have blessed to blood,
   poured out in streams more rich than you can think,
   my testament, the home and hope of men:
   Take the cup, take the cup, take the cup and drink.

3. This is the body raised to life and breath,
   this is the blood that sings again like wine,
   the scars that glow in sign of victory.
   Rejoice with me, for I have conquered death;   *Words: Luke Connaughton*
   Live in me, live in me, live and love in me.   *Music: Kevin Mayhew*

200

Thou art wor-thy, thou art wor-thy, thou art wor-thy, oh Lord, to receive glo-ry, glo-ry; and honour, glo-ry and

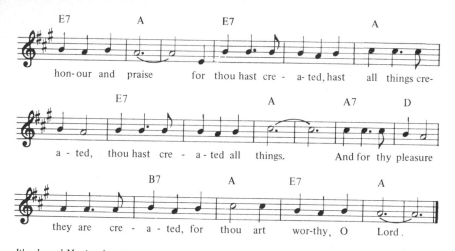

hon-our and praise for thou hast cre - a- ted, hast all things cre-

a - ted, thou hast cre - a - ted all things. And for thy pleasure

they are cre - a - ted, for thou art wor-thy, O Lord .

Words and Music: Anonymous

201

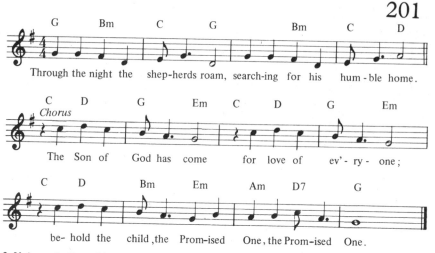

Through the night the shep-herds roam, search-ing for his hum - ble home.

Chorus

The Son of God has come for love of ev' - ry - one;

be- hold the child ,the Prom-ised One , the Prom-ised One .

2. Voices mingling with the breeze,
   sing in endless harmonies.

3. As they reach his lowly cave,
   bearing gifts they offer praise.

4. Can they know that through this child,
   man and God are reconciled?

Words and Music: Turloch Holmes

202

Bright stars of even-ing, high-est moun-tains, depths of the sea, all sing your song;
sour-ces of all the rush-ing riv-ers, sing of your God the whole day long.

Chorus
Ho-ly are you, Lord of all; help us to hear your sav-ing call!

Ho-ly are you, Lord of all; help us to hear your sav-ing call!

2. We who had strayed and we who wandered
   far from our Shepherd's holy fold.
   We have been rescued, brought in safely,
   in from the dark and deadly cold.

3. You burst the bars of evil prisons,
   freed from their cells all those who sinned.
   Death is led captive, fresh new vigour
   comes with the Pentecostal wind.

4. Praise to the Father, praise to Jesus,
   praise with a song the Holy Ghost,
   all of God's creatures, men and women,
   join to make up a mighty host!

Words: Willard F. Jabusch
Music: Ukranian melody

203

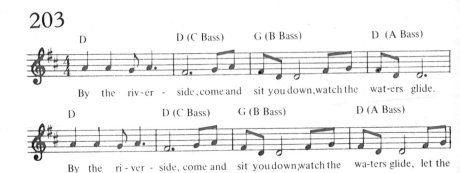

By the riv-er-side, come and sit you down, watch the wat-ers glide.

By the ri-ver-side, come and sit you down, watch the wa-ters glide, let the

care of ev' - ry day fade a - way on gentle river sands .

2. Maybe it's out here, what we're looking for,
   where the air is clear.
   Maybe it's out here, what we're looking for,
   where the air is clear,
   and the cares that weigh you down in the town
   don't matter anymore.

3. Maybe it's out here what we're looking for,
   something very clear.
   Maybe it's out here what we're looking for,
   something very clear,
   yes, a clear and obvious sign for our time,
   leaving no doubt at all.

4. Maybe he's out here, the one we're looking for,
   somewhere very near.
   Maybe he's out here, the one we're looking for,
   somewhere very near,
   speaking on the gentle air of his care;
   his love for evermore.

Words: Michael Cockett
Music: Malcolm Campbell-Carr

204

By the wa - ters, the wa - ters of Ba-by-lon,

we sat down and wept, and wept for thee Zi - on;

we re - mem-ber thee, re - mem - ber thee , re - mem-ber thee Zi - on.

2. On the willows, the willows of Babylon,
   we hung up our harps, for thee Zion;
   how can we sing, can we sing, sing of thee Zion.

3. There our captors, our captors from Babylon,
   tried to make us sing, and sing, of thee Zion;
   but we could not sing, we could not sing, we could not sing Zion.

Words: (based on Psalm 137) and   Music: Don McLean and Lee Hays

205

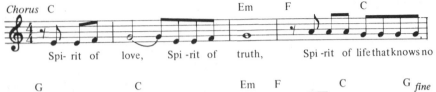

Spi- rit of love, Spi -rit of truth, Spi -rit of life that knows no

end. You are the truth, you are the love, you are the gift, the promised one.

1. This is the gift that was promised by the Son, free as a bird that can

glide up - on the wind. This is the hope that the world will all be one,

hope that he found in the darkness of the tomb.

2. This is the life that he laid down for his friends,
   life like a seed that can break the strongest chains.
   This is the peace that the world can never know,
   gift to all hearts that are troubled and afraid.

3. This is the truth that he offers to all men,
   fire that will burn like the constant golden sun.
   This is the love that will overcome his death,
   love we complete in the unity of man.

Words: Michael Cockett
Music: Malcolm Campbell-Carr

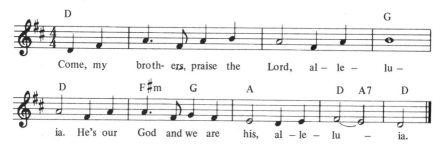

Come, my broth- ers, praise the Lord, al – le – lu –
ia. He's our God and we are his, al – le – lu – ia.

2. Come to him with songs of praise, alleluia.
Songs of praise, rejoice in him, alleluia.

3. For the Lord is a mighty God, alleluia.
He is king of all the world, alleluia.

4. In his hands are valleys deep, alleluia.
In his hands are mountain peaks, alleluia.

5. In his hands are all the seas, alleluia.
And the lands which he has made, alleluia.

6. Praise the Father, praise the Son, alleluia.
Praise the Spirit, the Holy One, alleluia.

Words and Music: Traditional

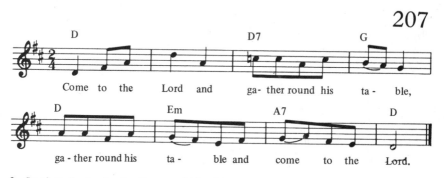

Come to the Lord and ga- ther round his ta - ble,
ga - ther round his ta - ble and come to the Lord.

2. Speak to the Lord and gather round his table.
Gather round his table and speak to the Lord.

3. Sing to the Lord and gather round his table.
Gather round his table and sing to the Lord.

4. Clap to the Lord and gather round his table.
Gather round his table and clap to the Lord.

5. Dance to the Lord and gather round his table.
Gather round his table and dance to the Lord.

Words and Music: Estelle White

208

What can we of - fer you Lord our God? How can we wor - ship you as you de - serve? We can on - ly of - fer what our lips do pro - claim We can on - ly of - fer you hum - ble acts of praise. But we of - fer this with Jes - us our bro - ther, Jes - us your Son. We join with him, glo - ry to you, O God! We join with him, glo - ry to you, O God!

2. What can we offer you, Lord our God?
   How can we thank you for all that you've done?
   We can only say it, Lord God, we thank you so.
   We can only try to live grateful lives, O Lord.
   But we offer this with Jesus, our brother, Jesus your Son.
   We join with him, our thanks to you, O God. (2)

3. What can we offer you, Lord our God?
   How do we prove we are truly sorry, Lord?
   We can say it often, God, sorry that we are.
   We can try to prove it, Lord, by the way we live.
   And we offer this with Jesus, our brother, Jesus, your Son.
   We join with him, forgive our sins, O God. (2)

4. What can we offer you, Lord our God?
   Dare we present you with another call for help?
   We just have to say it, Lord God, we need you so.
   We just have to beg you, Lord, take us by the hand.
   And we offer this with Jesus, our brother, Jesus, your Son.
   We join with him, Lord, we need you so. (2)

Words and Music: Tom Shelley

Lord, you know and stu - dy me and, Lord, you read my mind.

Lord, you know me through and through, you watch me all the time.

Close be - hind me, close in front, you shield me with your hand. Such

know-ledge is be - yond me, Lord; I can - not un - der - stand.

2. Lord, you know before I speak the words that I will say;
Lord, you know before I move each detail of my way.
I cannot escape you, Lord, your Spirit's ev'rywhere,
though heaven-bound or depths of hell, your presence will be there.

3. Though I try to run from you, across the raging sea
you will still be guiding there, your right hand holding me.
Dark will never cover me, nor daylight turn to night,
for dark is never black to you, and night becomes your light.

4. While inside my mother's womb you fashioned ev'ry part,
wrote the diary of my days before they had their start.
For these things I thank you, Lord – the mysteries I see,
the wonder, Lord, of all your works, the wonder, Lord, of me.

5. Lord, how hard to grasp your thoughts, how hard to understand!
I could no more count them, Lord, than I could count the sand.
Lord, just look now in my heart, probe me through and through,
and turn me, Lord, from evil ways, and lead me, Lord, to you.

Words and Music: Gillian Simpson

210

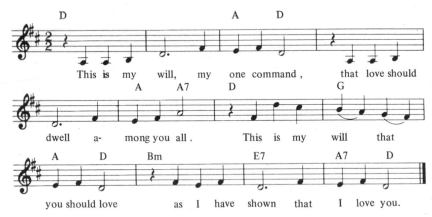

> D   A   D
>
> This is my will, my one command, that love should

> A   A7   D   G
>
> dwell a- mong you all. This is my will that

> A   D   Bm   E7   A7   D
>
> you should love as I have shown that I love you.

2. No greater love
   a man can have
   than that he die
   to save his friends.
   You are my friends
   if you obey
   all I command
   that you should do.

3. I call you now
   no longer slaves;
   no slave knows all
   his master does.
   I call you friends,
   for all I hear
   my Father say
   you hear from me.

4. You chose not me,
   but I chose you,
   that you should go
   and bear much fruit.
   I called you out
   that you in me
   should bear much fruit
   that will abide.

5. All that you ask
   my Father dear
   for my name's sake
   you shall receive.
   This is my will,
   my one command,
   that love should dwell
   in each, in all.

Words: James Quinn
Music: Traditional Irish Melody

211 *Chorus*

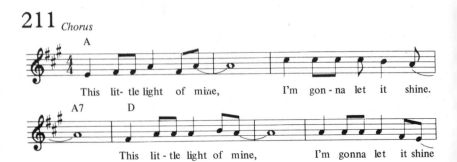

> A
>
> This lit- tle light of mine, I'm gon-na let it shine.

> A7   D
>
> This lit-tle light of mine, I'm gonna let it shine

This lit-tle light of mine, I'm gonna let it shine

let it shine, let it shine, let it shine.

1. The light that shines is the light of love.

lights the dark-ness from a-bove. It shines on me and it

shines on you, and shows what the power of love can do. I'm gonna

shine my light both far and near, I'm gonna shine my light both

bright and clear. Where there's a dark cor-ner in this land I'm gonna

let my lit-tle light shine.

2. On Monday he gave me the gift of love,
Tuesday peace came from above.
On Wednesday he told me to have more faith,
on Thursday he gave me a little more grace.
Friday he told me just to watch and pray,
Saturday he told me just what to say.
On Sunday he gave me the power divine
to let my little light shine.

Words and Music: Traditional

212

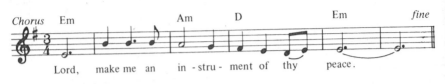

Chorus Em Am D Em *fine*

Lord, make me an in-stru-ment of thy peace.

G Em C D G Am

1. Where there is hat-red, let me sow love. Where there is in-ju-ry,

B7 D.C.

par-don.

G Em C D G Am

2. Where there is doubt, let me bring faith. Where there's de-spair,

B7 D.C.

hope.

G Em C D G Am

3. Where there is dark-ness, let me bring light. Where there is sad-ness,

B7 D.C.

joy.

4. Grant I may not seek to be con - soled as to con -

sole; not seek to be un - der - stood as to un - der -

stand; to be loved as to love .

5. For it is in giv - ing that we re - ceive, in

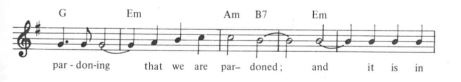

par - don-ing that we are par - doned; and it is in

dy - ing that we are born to e - ter - nal life.

Words (based on St. Francis of Assisi) and Music: Briege O'Hare

213

Come , Lord Je- sus , come. ——— Come, take my hands,
take them for your work. Take them for your ser- vice Lord.
Take them for your glo- ry, Lord, Come, Lord Je - sus,
come. Come , Lord Je- sus , take my hands.

2. Come, Lord Jesus, come.
   Come, take my eyes,
   may they shine with joy.
   Take them for your service, Lord.
   Take them for your glory, Lord.
   Come, Lord Jesus, come.
   Come, Lord Jesus, take my eyes.

3. Come, Lord Jesus, come.
   Come, take my lips,
   may they speak your truth.
   Take them for your service, Lord.
   Take them for your glory, Lord.
   Come, Lord Jesus, come.
   Come, Lord Jesus, take my lips.

4. Come, Lord Jesus, come.
   Come take my feet,
   may they walk your path.
   Take them for your service, Lord.
   Take them for your glory, Lord.
   Come, Lord Jesus, come.
   Come, Lord Jesus, take my feet.

5. Come, Lord Jesus, come.
   Come, take my heart,
   fill it with your love.
   Take it for your service, Lord.
   Take it for your glory, Lord.
   Come, Lord Jesus, come.
   Come, Lord Jesus, take my heart.

6. Come, Lord Jesus, come.
   Come, take my life,
   take it for your own.
   Take it for your service, Lord.
   Take it for your glory, Lord.
   Come, Lord Jesus, come.
   Come, Lord Jesus, take my life.

Words and Music: Kevin Mayhew

Mine eyes have seen the glory of the coming of the Lord. He is
trampling out the vintage where the grapes of wrath are stored. He has
loosed the fateful lightning of his terrible swift sword. His
truth is marching on. Glory, glory hallelujah!
Glory glory hallelujah! Glory, glory hallelujah! His truth is marching on.

2. I have seen him in the watchfires of a hundred circling camps.
They have gilded him an altar in the evening dews and damps.
I can read his righteous sentence by the dim and flaring lamps.
His day is marching on.

3. He has sounded forth the trumpet that shall never sound retreat.
He is sifting out the hearts of men before his judgement seat.
O, be swift, my soul, to answer him, be jubilant my feet!
Our God is marching on.

4. In the beauty of the lilies Christ was born across the sea
with a glory in his bosom that transfigures you and me.
As he died to make men holy, let us die to make men free.
Whilst God is marching on.

Words: Julia Howe
Music: Traditional American

215

Bless the Lord, oh my soul, bless the Lord, oh my soul, and all that is with-in me, bless his ho-ly Name.

2. Praise the Lord . . .

3. Love the Lord . . .   *Words and Music: Anonymous*

216

Bles-sed are my peo-ple, says the Lord. Bles-sed are my peo-ple, says the Lord. Come to me, friends of mine, come share my life di-vine, come to the ban-quet of the Lord.

2. Blessed are the lonely . . .   5. Blessed are the gentle . . .

3. Blessed are the humble . . .   6. Blessed are the hungry . . .

4. Blessed are the downcast . . .

Words (based on the Beatitudes) and Music: Kevin Mayhew

217

Bread from the earth, wine from the soil, A- dam made of

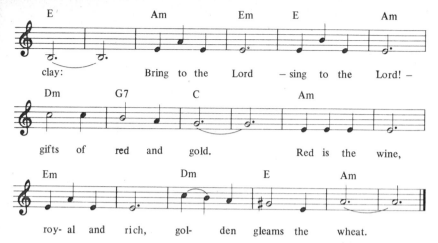

clay: Bring to the Lord — sing to the Lord! — gifts of red and gold. Red is the wine, roy- al and rich, gol- den gleams the wheat.

2. Fashioned from dust, what can you give, Man, so weak, so poor?
   Bring to the Lord — sing to the Lord! — what he gave to you:
   spirit of flame, mastering mind, body fine and proud.

3. Cry on his name, worship your God, all who dwell on earth.
   Bring to the Lord — sing to the Lord! — heart and voice and will.
   Father and Son, Spirit most high, worship three in one.

Words: Luke Connaughton
Music: Kevin Mayhew

218

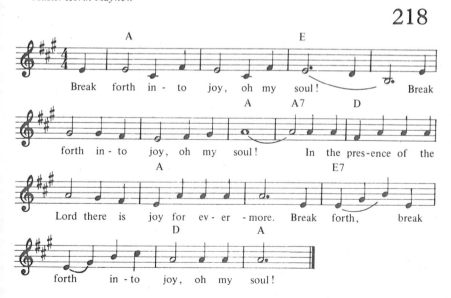

Break forth in - to joy, oh my soul! Break forth in - to joy, oh my soul! In the pres-ence of the Lord there is joy for ev - er -more. Break forth, break forth in - to joy, oh my soul!

Words and Music: Anonymous

219

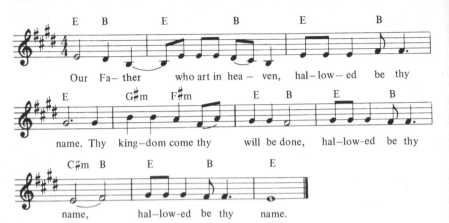

Our Fa— ther who art in hea — ven, hal—low— ed be thy name. Thy king—dom come thy will be done, hal—low-ed be thy name, hal—low-ed be thy name.

2. On earth as it is in heaven. . .
   Give us this day our daily bread. . .

3. Forgive us our trespasses. . .
   as we forgive those who trespass against us. . .

4. And lead us not into temptation. . .
   but deliver us from all that is evil. . .

5. For thine is the kingdom, the power and the glory. . .
   for ever, and forever and ever. . .

6. Amen, amen, it shall be so. . .
   Amen, amen, it shall be so. . .

Words and Music: Traditional Caribbean

220

Peace I leave with you, peace I give to you; not as the world gives peace, do I give.

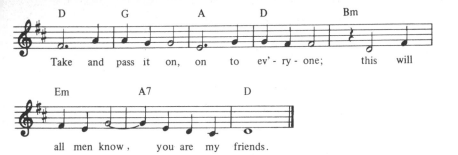

Take and pass it on, on to ev'-ry-one; this will all men know, you are my friends.

Words and Music: Peter Madden

221

Peace is flowing like a ri— ver, flow–ing out through you and me, spread–ing out in–to the des–ert, set – ting all the cap–tives free.

2. Love is flowing. . .

3. Joy is flowing. . .

4. Hope is flowing. . .

Words and Music: Anonymous

222 GEORDIE MASS

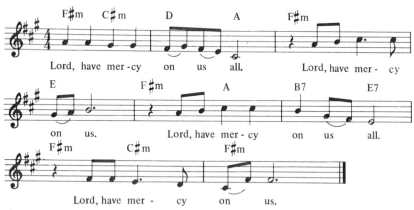

Lord, have mer-cy on us all. Lord, have mer - cy on us. Lord, have mer - cy on us all. Lord, have mer - cy on us.

Christ, have mercy on us all.
Christ, have mercy on us. (Repeat)
Lord, have mercy on us all.
Lord, have mercy on us. (Repeat)

Holy Holy Holy

Holy, holy, holy Lord
God of might and God of pow'r.
Glory fills all heav'n and earth.
Sing to him Hosanna!
Blessed is the one who comes
in the name of Christ our Lord.
Holy, holy, holy Lord.
Sing to him Hosanna!

Lamb of God

Lamb of God, you take our sins,
take away our sins, Lord.
So have mercy on us all,
so have mercy on us. (Repeat)

Lamb of God, you take our sins,
take away our sins, Lord.
Grant us peace, O grant us peace,
grant us peace for ever.

*Words and Music: Anthony Hamson
(adapted from an English folk melody)*

223 ISRAELI MASS

Lord, have mer - cy. Lord, have mer - cy. Lord, have mer-cy on us all. Lord, have mer -cy. Lord, have mer -cy Lord, have mercy on us all.

Christ, have mercy, Christ, have mercy.
Christ, have mercy on us all. (Repeat)
Lord, have mercy. Lord, have mercy.
Lord, have mercy on us all. (Repeat)

HOLY, HOLY, HOLY

Holy, holy, holy Lord
Lord of power, Lord of might.
Heav'n and earth are filled with glory.
Sing Hosanna evermore.

Blest and holy, blest and holy
he who comes from God on high.
Raise your voices, sing his glory,
praise his name for evermore.

LAMB OF GOD

Lamb of God, you take away the sin,
the sin of all the world.
Give us mercy, give us mercy,
give us mercy, Lamb of God. (Repeat)

Lamb of God, you take away the sin,
the sin of all the world.
Grant us peace, Lord, grant us peace,
Lord, grant us peace, O Lamb of God.

Words and Music: Anthony Hamson
(adapted from an Israeli folk melody)

MASS OF GOD'S PEOPLE **224**

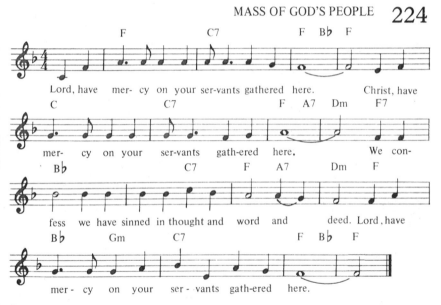

Lord, have mer-cy on your ser-vants gathered here. Christ, have mer-cy on your ser-vants gath-ered here. We con-fess we have sinned in thought and word and deed. Lord, have mer-cy on your ser-vants gath-ered here.

Sanctus

Holy, holy, holy Lord of pow'r and might,
earth and heaven sing hosanna in your praise.
He is blessed who comes in the name of the Lord.
Sing hosanna in the highest. Praise the Lord.

Agnus Dei

Lamb of God, you take the sin of all the world.
Lamb of God, you take the sin of all the world.
Show us mercy and grant us all the peace of Christ.
Lamb of God, you take the sin of all the world.

Words and Music: Adapted from traditional sources by Kevin Mayhew

225

Lord, we pray for gol- den peace, peace all o- ver the
land, May all men dwell in lib- er- ty, all
walk- ing hand in hand. Ban- ish fear and ig- nor- ance,
hun- ger, thirst and pain. Ban- ish hate and pov- er- ty, let
no man live in vain, let no man live in vain.

2. Keep all men for ever one,
   one in love and in grace.
   And wipe away all war and strife,
   give freedom to each race.

3. Let your justice reign supreme.
   righteousness always done.
   Let goodness rule the hearts of men
   and evil overcome.

Words and Music: Sebastian Temple

At Beth-le-hem she bore her Son and gave the world a King, yet poor and hum-ble was that place where an-gel hosts did sing.

Chorus
She will show us the Pro-mised One, she will show us the Pro-mised One; Oh, Mo-ther of Je-sus, be so kind as to show us the Pro-mised One.

2. At Nazareth she heard the voice
   of Gabriel to say:
   "Oh Mary, you are full of grace,
   the Lord's with you today!"

3. At Cana when the wine ran out
   she told him of the case,
   and Jesus did a wond'rous thing,
   his kindness filled that place.

4. At Golgotha she felt the pain
   and cross her Son did bear;
   they took his broken body down;
   her arms received him there.

5. In heaven where she reigns as queen
   she keeps a mother's heart;
   she sides with all who struggle here,
   and takes the sinner's part.

Words: Willard F. Jabusch
Music: American melody

227

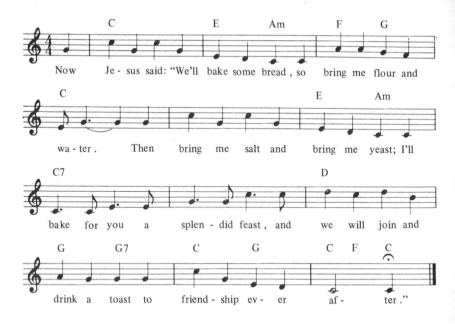

C   E   Am   F   G

Now Je-sus said: "We'll bake some bread, so bring me flour and

C   E   Am

wa-ter. Then bring me salt and bring me yeast; I'll

C7   D

bake for you a splen-did feast, and we will join and

G   G7   C   G   C F C

drink a toast to friend-ship ev-er af-ter."

2. They found the flour, they found the salt,
   they found a jug of water.
   But, though they searched around the town,
   an ounce of yeast could not be found.
   They came to him with eyes cast down
   and told him of their failure.

3. Then Jesus said: "Do not be sad,
   we'll mix the flour and water.
   And though we bake unleavened bread,
   if you will be the yeast instead,
   the bread will rise up from the dead
   and feed you ever after."

Words: Michael Cockett
Music: Kevin Mayhew

228

C   G   C

My Lord, my Mas-ter, my God, my Sa-viour, Lord of

G   C   F

earth, Lord of hea-ven, I praise you now. Be my food for the

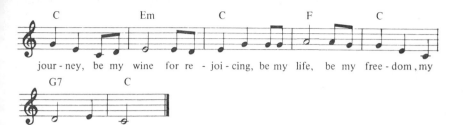

jour - ney, be my wine for re - joi - cing, be my life, be my free - dom, my

Lord, my God.

2. My Lord, my Master, my God, my Saviour,
   Lord of earth, Lord of heaven, I praise you now.
   Be my food for the journey, be my wine for rejoicing,
   be my truth, be my wisdom,
   my Lord, my God.

3. My Lord, my Master, my God, my Saviour,
   Lord of earth, Lord of heaven, I praise you now.
   Be my food for the journey, be my wine for rejoicing,
   be my peace, be my vision,
   my Lord, my God.

Words: Kevin Mayhew
Music: Traditional Scottish melody

229

Praise him, praise him, praise him in the morn-ing
praise him in the noon-time. Praise him, praise him,
praise him when the sun goes down.

2. Love him. . . 4. Serve him. . .

3. Trust him. . . 5. Jesus. . . *Words and Music: Anonymous*

230

*This song may be performed either in unison
repeating it as many times as needed, or as a round.
The song ends on the first note – praise.*

Praise to the Lord our – God, let us sing to–gether, lif–ting our hearts and our

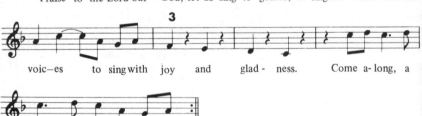

voic–es to sing with joy and glad - ness. Come a-long, a

long, a- long, and sing with

Words: Estelle White
Music: Unknown

INDEX OF FIRST LINES

INDEX OF USES

ACKNOWLEDGMENTS

he publishers wish to express their gratitude to the following for permission to include opyright material in this book:

'orth American Liturgy Resources for *Alleluia. We will hear your Word.*

halom Community for *O living water* and *I sing a song to you, Lord* © copyright, 1974, y Shalom Community, 1504 Polk, Wichita Falls, Texas 76309. All rights reserved. Used ith permission.

wald Bash for *Where shall we find bread.*

illian Simpson for *God gave his Son for sinful men; Like the stars in the sky; Jesus, the ealer; Lord, you know and study me; Oh Lord my God, how great you are; Oh when the irit comes.*

ev. Damian Webb for *One, one, eternal one* and *Look upon our offerings.*

ev. Willard F. Jabusch for *All this world belongs to Jesus; Many times I have turned; ail Mary, Mother of our God; Now watch for God's coming; He is risen, tell the story; right stars of evening; The King of Glory comes; Whatsoever you do; Open your ears.*

S. Paluch Company of Illinois, U.S.A., for *What a joy* and *At Bethlehem she bore her son.*

'orld Library Publications of Cincinnati for *Take our bread.*

sef Weinberger Ltd. for *Lord, Jesus Christ; All creation bless the Lord; O Lord, all the orld belongs to you* and *At the name of Jesus.*

ranciscan Communications Center of Los Angeles for *All that I am; Glorious God, King f creation; Take my hands; The Mass is ended; Leave it in the hands of the Lord; Happy e man; Make me a channel of your peace; Faith, hope and charity; Sing praises to the ving God; Lord, we pray for golden peace* and *Good Lady Poverty.*

usical Gospel Outreach for *Colours of Day.*

'orld Records Europe for *Holy, holy, holy.*

eoffrey Chapman Ltd. for *Christ be beside me* and *This is my will.*

xford University Press for *Now the green blade riseth* from 'The Oxford book of Carols' nd *God is love* from 'Songs of Praise'.

lba House Communications for *What can we offer you, Lord.*

he copyright of the following songs is vested in Kevin Mayhew Ltd: 2, 3, 4, 5, 6, 10, 11, 2, 13, 14, 16, 18, 19, 20, 21, 22, 23, 25, 29, 31, 33, 37, 38, 39, 44, 45, 47, 49, 51, 52, 6, 57, 59, 60, 62, 67, 70, 71, 72, 76, 79, 80, 81, 82, 85, 87, 88, 90, 91, 94, 97, 99, 101, 04, 106, 107, 109, 111, 112, 115, 116, 118, 119, 120, 121, 122, 123, 124, 127, 129, 30, 131, 132, 134, 135, 136, 137, 138, 140, 141, 142, 144, 145, 146, 149, 150, 151, 52, 155, 156, 157, 159, 161, 162, 164, 165, 167, 169, 170, 174, 176, 178, 179, 182, 83, 184, 189, 190, 191, 193, 195, 197, 199, 201, 203, 205, 207, 212, 213, 216, 217, 20, 222, 223, 224, 227, 228, 230.

very effort has been made to contact the owners of copyright material and we hope that o copyright has been infringed. Pardon is sought and apology made if the contrary be the ase, and a correction will be made in any reprint of the book.